THE PUBLIC CALLS IT SPORT

THE PUBLIC CALLS IT SPORT

BY

Harry Wismer

Prentice-Hall, Inc., Englewood Cliffs, N. J.

The Public Calls It Sport
by Harry Wismer

Library of Congress Catalog Card Number: 65-27499

Printed in the United States of America

T   73718

Prentice-Hall International, Inc., London
Prentice-Hall of Australia, Pty., Ltd., Sydney
Prentice-Hall of Canada, Ltd., Toronto
Prentice-Hall of India (Private) Ltd., New Delhi
Prentice-Hall of Japan, Inc., Tokyo

*To my lovely wife Mary, for her patience and understanding;
and to George Halas, for his friendship and inspiration.*

ACKNOWLEDGMENT

I want to pay a tremendous vote of thanks to George Flynn, my editor at Prentice-Hall and his colleagues. Without their talents and assistance, this book could not have been written.

CONTENTS

Contents

THE PUBLIC CALLS IT SPORT

INTRODUCTION

The guards, like two matched Percherons, pull out of the line, leading the ball carrier to the right. From his defensive spot, the cornerback, eyes bulging at the sight of this mass of humanity bearing down on him, moves up to stop the play. He hurls himself at the blockers but is obliterated, his helmet flying off from the impact. Twenty yards downfield the ball carrier is stopped by the converging safety men, one hitting him at the knees, the other high around the shoulders. Up field, the cornerback, helmet in hand, moves slowly to the sidelines.

The game is pro football. It is violent, brutal, and the fans love it—huge men battering other huge men. But it's more; it's a ballet of ends and defensive backs, a chess match between coaches and quarterbacks. It's hand-to-hand combat between defensive ends and protecting blockers. Unlike the Roman gladiators, these modern combatants wear plastic helmets and tear-free jerseys. They don't carry a trident or spear, but their heavily bandaged forearms and elbows seem just as lethal.

The maneuvering, the toughness, and the violence carry over to another arena, one the fan never sees. This is the domain of the men who, from oak-paneled offices, control the game, the

1

players and coaches on the field, the broadcasters in the booth; it's the world of the owners of pro football franchises.

In many respects, the behind-the-scenes game is even tougher, places a greater premium on guile than the game itself. Behind the oaken doors there is no referee to call clipping, no umpire to call holding, and as I found out, often no teammates to lean on, no running guards to clear your path. The game I played was pro football—the business side of the sport—for thirty years. I thought I knew my way around but I made a fundamental mistake when I agreed to help start the American Football League—I aligned myself with amateurs, and I assumed that we were one for all and all for one. These mistakes would cost me two million dollars.

First as an errand boy, then as a broadcaster and finally as a part owner of the Detroit Lions from 1947-1964; and of the Washington Redskins from 1950-1960, this was my business. And I was a hustler; I always have been a hustler and I'm proud of it. No one ever gave me anything; what I made I made through my own efforts. I broke some rules, trod on some toes, gambled and risked. I thought I had all the answers. I hadn't learned that no matter how good you think you are, how shrewd you are, there is always someone down the block, across the street, in the next town, who is a little bit better, shrewder, more ruthless. I hadn't learned, though I should have known, that amateurs and dilettantes in any field are unpredictable, uncertain quantities. I went into the AFL confident and with my eyes open. My co-owners needed me to start the New York franchise, otherwise there would have been no AFL, no grand stadium in Flushing Meadows. I brought them TV experience, publicity, and helped them establish three of their most stable franchises. Yet when I needed help, financial help, they turned their backs; and in the wings, ready to administer the *coup de grace*, stood one of my own ilk, a hustler like myself, the guy down the block, who bruised my own toes and picked up my team.

Like the game of pro football itself, this book may leave some bruises and some aches. It couldn't be written any other way. The game on the field is tough; so is the business.

PART I

THE EARLY YEARS

I learned early to respect money and the power and influence it commands at about the same time I was learning that athletics are a great equalizer and a ready entré for any gifted and ambitious youth. It's not that poverty stalked my childhood. My father was general manager of the Higers Clothing Store in Port Huron, Michigan, and the small white house with the green shutters at 1107 Howard Street was a comfortable and happy place. But there was another part of Port Huron, the part inhabited by my two close friends, Fred and Tyler Reggin, whose father owned the Mueller Brass Company, the largest business establishment in town.

The Reggins were treated with deference and respect and moved about town with calm assurance and confidence. As a friend of the Reggin boys, as their teammate at George Washington Junior High, I passed through doors that otherwise would have been closed to me, received the same adulation as a local sports celebrity, saw how irrresistible the combination of money and a sports reputation could be. I enjoyed the experience. I don't think many kids would have been immune to it.

I can remember, as a kid, nailing a tin can to the wall of the porch my father had added to our house and sitting for hours,

flipping a tennis ball through it. It seemed I was always swing-
ing a bat or throwing or catching a ball.

My friends and I had a bottomless appetite for sports. Baseball was the king of sports when I was young and the feats of
Ruth, Cobb, Johnson, and Hornsby were familiar to every boy
in the land. My particular favorite was Ty Cobb, the great
Detroit Tiger outfielder.

I saw Cobb play many times at Navin Field in Detroit, site
of the present Tiger Stadium. My Dad and I would drive down
from Port Huron and I'll never forget the slashing, hell-for-
leather style that was Cobb's trademark. His toughness and
desire were an inspiration.

But if baseball was the national pastime, college football,
Big Ten style, was king in the Midwest. I played all sports as a
youngster but my favorite was football, my favorite team, Notre
Dame. Those were the days of the Four Horsemen, George
Gipp, and the great Rockne. At Michigan, the immortal
Fielding H. Yost was turning out his "Champions of the West"
led by Benny Friedman and Benny Oosterban. Red Grange was
at Illinois, Duke Slater at Iowa, Walter Eckersall at Chicago.

I played football, basketball, and baseball at George Washington Junior High, and captained the basketball team to the
state title. After junior high I received an athletic scholarship to
St. John's Military Academy in Delafield, Wisconsin. There I
won eight letters in football, basketball, baseball, and track.

Upon graduation in June of 1932, I began to shop around for
a college athletic scholarship. None of the Big Ten schools
showed any particular interest in me, probably because I was
relatively small. I had played quarterback and weighed only
160. So I went south, hitchhiking. It was easy to get rides then.
There were no superhighways and no souped-up limousines to
dodge. The depression was on, and people who had cars helped
out those who didn't. In my pocket I had a letter of introduc-

tion to Charlie Bachman, coach at the University of Florida, from my high school coach. After trying and failing at Vanderbilt and Georgia, I finally arrived at Gainesville and met Bachman. He wasn't overenthusiastic about my potential, but he knew I had been schooled in midwestern football and probably could play well enough to make the freshman team. I got the ride—room, board, tuition, books, and odd jobs to keep me in spending money.

At Florida I roomed at the SAE house with George Smathers, varsity left end, and Phil Graham. The three of us became fast friends, and George and I still are. Phil, who became publisher of the *Washington Post* and *Newsweek* magazine, died in 1963. Smathers entered politics and has served the state of Florida well for a number of years as United States Senator.

I went back to Port Huron during the Christmas holidays and, though I did not know it, I had spent not only my first but my last semester at Florida. While home I had lunch with Sam McCool, head of the Associated Press in Lansing, who told me during the course of the meal that Jimmy Crowley, coach at Michigan State, was quitting to take the coaching job at Fordham. McCool said the story wouldn't break until after the first of the year and that the job was wide open. Sam's source at State was Ralph Young, the athletic director and his close friend.

Actually, Sam had gotten in touch with me about an entirely different matter. He was in love with Florence Gleason, sister of my good friend Bill Gleason. Florence wasn't giving Sam much of a tumble and Sam asked me if I would put in a good word for him. I saw Florence a few days later and did put in a plug for Sam. I don't know how much my one attempt as a marriage broker had to do with it, but Sam and Florence eventually were married.

I knew Bachman was in trouble at Florida because he had

had three straight losing seasons and the alumni and news-
papers were after his job. Bachman was a good coach. Knute
Rockne considered him the most promising coaching prospect
among all his former players. I felt that Bachman should apply
for the State job. I discussed it with McCool and he thought
Bachman, as a Rockne man and nationally known, would stand
a good chance.

I went to Bachman after I returned to school to tell him
about the State job. That same day the news about Crowley's
resignation broke, and within a few days almost 100 applications had deluged Ralph Young at State. I convinced Bachman
to apply for the position and he did. However, I also called
Sam McCool to tell him Bachman had applied, reminded him
about the favor I had done for him, and asked him to do what
he could for Bachman. Sam never told me what he did to help,
but a week or so later, Bachman and Young agreed on terms and
Bachman got the job. As coach, he asked me if I would like to
return to my home state and play football at Michigan State.

I went back with Bachman and played on his freshman team
that fall. The next year I was on the varsity as third-string
quarterback and that year, Bachman's varsity Spartans beat
mighty Michigan, coached by Harry Kipke, 16-0, one of the
great football victories in State's illustrious sports history. Beating Michigan in those days was quite a feat and guaranteed
Bachman a long stay at Michigan State.

Following the victory over Michigan, State was to play
Carnegie Tech at Lansing and the game was to be broadcast
nationally by Bill Stern and Graham McNamee, the two top
sports broadcasters in the country. I had been injured during
practice the week of the Michigan game, and as practice began
for Carnegie Tech, Bachman took me aside and asked me if I
wanted to give up football and take over the sports-broadcast-
ing spot for the school network. The university had a 5,000-watt
transmitter and its station, WKAR, reached all over Michigan. I

was reluctant to give up football, but I had been pretty well banged up and the school doctors had advised me to quit. Maybe broadcasting would be fun. Anyway, it would be the next best thing to being on the field.

Bachman made arrangements for me to work in the booth so I could see how Stern and McNamee worked. Both men were friendly, but whereas Stern was very businesslike and meticulous in his preparation, McNamee was seemingly casual and unconcerned. It didn't take me long to realize that both of them were past masters at the broadcasting game, although during the first half, I couldn't believe that I was watching the same game they were describing. Stern made even the simplest line buck sound like an 80-yard run. McNamee would rhapsodize over every detail—the color of the sky, the color of the uniforms, the color of the grass, although he was more matter-of-fact than Stern in describing the action on the field. But as the game wore on I began to realize that both were giving the listener a vivid, colorful account of what was going on, but in terms that lent great excitement to the game. Michigan State won the game and it was a rather dull affair, but listening to Stern and McNamee I came to understand that they made the game and the day seem much more exciting to their listeners than it really was.

I was hooked. To be able to tell people about a game was one thing, but to make it come alive with action, drama, and tension, even if there wasn't any, was an art, an art I wanted to master. After seeing Stern and McNamee at work, I told Bachman I was his man. I would take the job as sports broadcaster for WKAR.

In June of 1935, I began looking for more to do besides broadcasting for the school. I wanted to stay with sports but with school closed down for the summer vacation I had to come up with something to keep me busy. My solution was simple: I would run Charlie Bachman for coach of the College All-Stars.

In 1934, Arch Ward, sports editor of the *Chicago Tribune*, introduced the first College All-Star game, played between the top collegiate seniors of the past season coached by Nobel Kizer of Purdue, and the champions of the National Football League, the Chicago Bears. Ward had originated the baseball All-Star game between the stars of the National League and the American League that previous summer, in July 1933, in conjunction with the World's Fair in Chicago. The baseball game was a success and convinced Ward that the All-Star football extravaganza in August would be equally attractive. In 1935, Ward hit on the idea of letting fans across the nation elect the coach. It proved to be a shrewd move, as millions of votes were cast through the *Tribune* and affiliated outlets.

Getting Bachman elected took more than just my voice over WKAR and the Bachman fans in Michigan. Being relatively isolated in Lansing didn't help either. I needed a national campaign and money to run one. There was one place to go for money in Michigan and that was to Detroit. The auto capital of the world had the ingredients I needed to put Bachman in, but I didn't know anyone there who had money, connections, or influence. But I had heard about one man who seemed to me to be as promotion-conscious as I was—George "Dick" Richards, owner of the Detroit Lions. Richards had made a fortune as an automobile dealer in Ohio and had come to Detroit in the early Thirties seeking new worlds to conquer. He bought the Portsmouth, Ohio, Spartans in 1933, brought them to Detroit, dressed them in Honolulu blue jerseys, and renamed them the Lions.

I called Richards and told him what I wanted to do, explained to him the process of electing the All-Star coach, and asked for his help. He agreed to talk it over and asked Bachman and me to meet with him in Detroit. We did and Richards quickly saw the publicity possibilities in our scheme. His main interests were in promoting football, the professional variety in Detroit, and in establishing a pipeline to the Michigan State campus through which to pump future Lions to Detroit.

Bachman would have a tough job trying to win the election because Frank Thomas, the Alabama coach, was considered a shoo-in. His Rose Bowl team, led by Dixie Howell, Don Hutson, and Paul "Bear" Bryant, had captured the nation's fancy with its smashing victory over Stanford in the Rose Bowl the preceding New Year's Day. Thomas was a master coach, but with Richards' help maybe Bachman could come close.

Since anyone could vote, Richards got some of his Lion players to fill in ballots with names from the Detroit phone book. Many of the players were living at Webster Hall, a boarding house near the Fisher building where Richards' WJR studios were located. Such known greats as Ace Gutowsky, George Christenson, and others would sit in their rooms, clad only in their undershorts, and fill in the ballots. I can still recall the look of intense concentration on Gutowsky's face as he wrote, "I, Suzi Schoenberg of Grand River, vote for Charles Bachman." Even Clarke Hinkle, the great Green Bay Packer fullback, helped. He was living at Webster and got a big kick out of the operation. These votes, plus others that we received from around the state, pushed Bachman into second place behind Thomas in the final tabulation. Then fate, or luck, or what-have-you intervened. Thomas came down with the gout just before the game and Bachman took over and coached the All-Stars. They didn't win: the Bears beat them 5-0—but I had helped put Bachman in and I'd profited both from the All-Star experience and from meeting Dick Richards.

Richards was the first important businessman I had ever worked closely with. His holdings, besides his automobile dealership, included three of the largest radio stations in the country —WJR in Detroit, WGAR in Cleveland, and KMPC in Los Angeles. But of all his interests, the Detroit Lions commanded most of his attention. They had rewarded their owner's efforts handsomely by winning their first NFL championship in 1935.

It was during one of the Lions games at Titan Stadium on the campus at the University of Detroit that Richards asked me to take over as field announcer for the Lions. Richards loved color, so when I introduced the Lion players before the game, I'd say, "And here is Dutch Clark, the greatest quarterback that ever lived," or, "Here is Ace Gutowsky, the finest fullback in football." I had learned early that objectivity was a luxury that broadcasters could not afford. Clark was indeed one of the all time greats and Gutowsky deserved his accolade, but when you represent the owner, his players and his team are always the best, no matter what, because the man who pays the tab says they are. Richards had fired my predecessor for lack of color and I was going to show him that I could enliven even the field announcements.

He liked my style and offered me a job as sports announcer for WJR. I took it. I was still attending college, so I'd hitchhike to Detroit every evening for the 10:15 P.M. show and hitchhike back, a round trip of about 170 miles. Richards thought I was crazy; he was paying me good money and didn't see any reason why I should continue in school. He finally made it clear that I would either have to devote full time to my announcing or quit. Since he was a self-made man without a college degree, he couldn't see why I wanted a degree when I was doing better at WJR than most college graduates in 1935. And, as usual, he was right. I quit college and joined WJR full time. Within one year I was making $20,000 and by the time I was twenty-five I grossed over $100,000. In addition to my nightly show for WJR, I soon became the play-by-play announcer of the Lions, and on Saturday I'd travel the Midwest covering the Big Ten.

More and more I became involved with Richards, the Lions, and the NFL. Richards often asked me to represent him at league meetings, and it was at these meetings that my education in the business of pro football began. I'd gone to college to get a degree to go into business, but after quitting college I got the best education possible. My business was sports announcing, and pro football and league meetings were my seminars.

Pro football in the Thirties was an emerging sport. In the Twenties it had struggled to stay alive, supported mainly by small towns across the East and Midwest. But, by the Thirties the sport had begun to outgrow Rock Island and Portsmouth and Canton and Massillon. They had given their fields and their men to the sport, nursed it as it grew, had given the game the backbone it needed to compete in the "big city." The history of pro football in these towns is rich with excitement, humor, and legendary figures. The lessons learned served pro football well.

Breaking into the highly competitive big-city sports market was no easy task for the young league. Richards was one of the first owners to realize that the game needed the support of big business in the cities they played in and he lined up many influential people in Detroit to serve on the Lions' board of directors.

The men who ran the NFL in the Thirties were tough, intelligent, and spirited. League meetings sometimes resembled a longshoremen's union meeting. The meeting room was never plush, just an inexpensive suite on the small side. Only the owners and the few general managers were there plus a lawyer or two for those who could afford one. More often than not the agenda was forgotten as one after the other would jump to his feet and shout his views. And if he couldn't see his antagonist through the smoke, at least he knew he was heard.

The commissioner then, as in the Twenties, was Joe Carr, a slight, bespectacled man who had been with the League since 1921. Carr made many contributions to the game during his tenure, but unfortunately has never received the publicity due him, probably because he was overshadowed by the owners. And after meeting these owners and seeing them in action, seeing Marshall and Halas go at it, one wonders if any commissioner, even another Judge Landis, could have managed them.

Some of these owners are still around, but I remember them as I first saw them, carving out a place for professional football in American sports. Men like this would have been leaders in any field at any period of history. A rollcall of their names reads like a *Who's Who* of Football—George Halas of the Chicago Bears, George Marshall of the Washington Redskins, Curly Lambeau of the Green Bay Packers, Tim Mara of the New York Giants, Dick Richards of the Detroit Lions, Charlie Bidwill of the Chicago Cardinals, Art Rooney of the Pittsburgh Steelers, Bert Bell of the Philadelphia Eagles, and Dan Topping of the Brooklyn Dodgers.

The name George Halas stands for pro football; it is synonymous with leadership and championship. More than any man, Halas has left his mark on this sport; and his team, the Chicago Bears, was the first glamor team of pro football, the team that comes immediately to mind when you mention greatness in professional football.

I broadcast the 1940 regular season game between the Bears and the Redskins, which the Bears lost 7-3. After the game, Halas had some critical remarks to make about the officiating. The next day the Washington papers carried Halas' statements, and George Marshall reacted by dubbing Halas and the Bears "crybabies." I spent the week following that game with Halas and was with him and the coaches as they reviewed the films of the loss. They were to play the same team for the championship back in D.C. Halas and the Bears were primed for that one —Marshall's label still rankled. You know the result. The Bears slaughtered the 'Skins 73-0 in the greatest single exhibition of perfection in the history of football. Through Halas, I was assigned to broadcast the game, and afterward I asked George why he let the score run to such proportions. I'll never forget his words: "Marshall deserved it and I couldn't hold the team back, even if I wanted to."

In 1947, George and I were having dinner in the Pump Room at the Ambassador East Hotel in Chicago. Halas' old colleague and close friend, Charles Bidwill, owner of the Chicago Cardinals, lay near death in the hospital. During the lunch the waiter brought a phone to our table and told George there was a call for him. George picked up the receiver, said "hello" and listened. He put down the receiver, looked at me, nodded, and began to cry. Bidwill was dead. Shrewd, tough, and relentless as he was, Halas couldn't bear the loss of a friend. My testimonial to Halas means nothing. The real tribute comes each year when former Bears return to Chicago to pay homage to the man who taught and inspired them.

Although George Preston Marshall was not one of pro football's pioneers, his contributions to the sport are many. Marshall joined the NFL in 1932 when he bought the Boston Braves, later renamed the Redskins. Actually his wife, the "Orchid Lady" of movie fame, Corinne Griffith, got the deal off the ground. Marshall stayed in Boston until 1936, when his losses, over $85,000, became too great to take. He moved the franchise to Washington, even though his Redskins won the Eastern title in 1936. They played the championship game against the Green Bay Packers in New York while in transit to Washington and lost, 21-6. In his heyday Marshall was one of the most colorful, controversial, and exciting persons in the history of pro football. On Sunday evenings after a Redskin home game, George and his wife Corinne would go to the Blue Room of the Shoreham Hotel for dinner. Marshall would time his entrance to be sure that Barney Breskin and his orchestra would be on the bandstand playing. Then, he and Corinne would enter the room and Breskin would stop the music, tap twice with his baton, and then lead the orchestra in "Hail To The Redskins." George and Corinne would walk slowly through the room to their table by the bandstand as the men in the room stood and applauded. George would sit at his special table, reminding me a little of FDR as he smiled and waved, obviously immensely pleased at what was essentially a staged performance, although a very effective one as Marshall played it. Corinne had helped Barney

Breskin write "Hail To The Redskins." To my way of thinking, Corinne was really the one who made George the success he was. She had money and brains and connections and carried George along in her wake.

It was Marshall who thought up the idea for the Pro Bowl game. He and Halas and Bell sold the other owners on the plan and then they asked me to sell it to TV. In 1951 the first game was played in Los Angeles. Actually, there had been an All-Star game between the champions of the league and a collection of stars from the rest of the league teams as far back as 1938, but the event had been cancelled after the 1942 game.

I was to broadcast that first Pro Bowl game and had checked in at the Beverly Hills Hotel. The morning of the game I was awakened about 4 A.M. by a telephone call. It was Marshall, calling from Washington, where it was 7 A.M. George apologized for waking me so early and launched right into his pitch. "Harry, here's what you do. As soon as you begin the game broadcast, mention that this great sports spectacle is the brainchild of George Preston Marshall, owner of the Washington Redskins, and repeat it about five times during the game." Like a good and faithful announcer should, I followed instructions.

The team that beat Marshall's wandering tribe for the championship in 1936 was founded by a twenty-one year old quarterback who had quit Knute Rockne and Notre Dame in 1919 and started his own team; an outfit called the Green Bay Packers. Earl "Curly" Lambeau's team was actually owned by the citizens of Green Bay, who in 1923 put up the money for Lambeau to keep operating. For their money they were given nonprofit stock and decades of great football. Curly's contribution to pro football lies mainly in his abilities as a coach and the refinements he added to the passing game. His Packer teams were the first to exploit the forward pass and to add that exciting dimension to football.

In January of 1961, after my first season with my Titans in

New York, I asked Curly to come to New York to spend a few weeks with me. He stayed with me and we talked about football and reminisced about the great days of Hutson and Isbell. I offered Curly the position as Executive Vice President of the New York Titans in the American Football League and Curly turned me down. He said he had made enough money to live comfortably and he didn't think he wanted to get involved in the tough task of starting a new football league. Curly said, "Harry, all of us who grew up in the NFL had only our franchises to keep us going. We didn't have any rich man's sons and you know that you can't trust them when the going gets tough."

Curly visited the Polo Grounds with me and told me that unless I got my team out of there I was doomed. He said that the new stadium had better be completed soon. Curly really doubted that the American Football League would survive and he didn't want to take the chance of expending so much energy on something that had so few possibilities. He was a dear, wonderful friend and I will never forget our associations. He died June 1, 1965 and the sports world is the worse for it.

Tim Mara bought the New York Giants franchise in 1925 from Joe Carr for $2,500, through the good offices of Jimmy Jemial, syndicated columnist of the *New York Daily News*. Next to the purchase of Manhattan by Peter Stuyvesant, it ranks as the best financial deal in New York history. Mara was a bookmaker of the legalized English type, an honorable vocation in those days, and he knew any franchise in New York for any sport was worth $2,500. Mara's love for football carried the Giants when they didn't draw flies to the Polo Grounds. He spent money to bring the best players to New York, convinced that a quality product would be supported by New Yorkers. He was right, but there were many days when only Mara's faith in the game and his stubborn resolve kept the Giants going.

Tim Mara made his money booking bets. Art Rooney made money betting. Art reportedly won $256,000 at the Saratoga

race track in 1927. Rooney joined the NFL in 1933 when he took
Joe Carr up on the challenge to put together some of the semi-
pro players in the Pittsburgh area and join the real pros. Art
was an exceptional, wonderful athlete and had received an offer
to play at Notre Dame, had tryouts with two major league
baseball clubs, and as an amateur boxer, once defeated Sammy
Mossberg, the Olympic welterweight champion. Rooney was
the first owner I knew who gambled heavily. Dick Richards
also was a big bettor.

Charlie Bidwill bought the Chicago Cardinals in 1933, the
same year that Art Rooney was coming in with Pittsburgh and
Bell was entering with the Eagles. To me he was the most
colorful of the owners, a cheerful and expansive man. Charlie
had a controlling interest in the Hawthorne race track in
Chicago and also was part owner of the Bears. Legislatively,
Bidwill didn't make any great contributions to pro football, but
his charm and wit kept many a league meeting from becoming
a brawl.

In 1933, the National Football League was joined by one
Bert Bell. Bell, along with Lud Wray, had taken over the franchise of the old Frankfort Yellow Jackets and renamed them
the Philadelphia Eagles. This new owner was to bring much
more than his team to this sport. Bert Bell was to be the architect of growth in pro football through his far-seeing innovations.

Dan Topping bought the Brooklyn franchise in 1934 and
joined the NFL, along with Richards, that year. Topping's
franchise always had a tough go, and he would later leave the
NFL and become a key owner in the All America Football
Conference. He was a quiet, calculating, though friendly man
who, after the collapse of the AAFC, became the co-owner of
the New York Yankees baseball team. Topping's financial support in the early years came from his then wife, the famed
skating star, Sonja Henie.

In 1926 Joe Carr put through the rule that no professional team could sign a college player until that player's class had graduated. This sensible rule protected the college teams from raids by the NFL and established the background for the fine relationship with the collegians that the NFL enjoys today.

The next major change in the rules came in 1932. Up to that time, a pass had to be thrown from at least five yards back of the line of scrimmage. The Packers, under Lambeau, had made the forward pass an integral part of the game and other teams were becoming increasingly pass-conscious. The five-yard rule created considerable confusion among officials and intense controversy; and Lambeau, along with Halas and Marshall, led the fight to have this rule dropped, to permit the passer to throw from anywhere behind the scrimmage line. The change carried and pro football opened up. The Packers, meanwhile, had signed Don Hutson, a pass-catching magician, who along with passers Arnie Herber and Cecil Isbell carried the Packers to many successful seasons. Marshall and Halas also benefitted from the new rule, as did all of pro football, for in 1937 the great Sammy Baugh joined the Redskins and two years later Sid Luckman came to the Bears.

The passing rule and the prohibition on signing college players before graduation of their class did much to solidify and open up pro football. But if one bit of legislation helped the game most, it was the draft. Football historians credit Bert Bell with proposing the draft, and it, more than any other single factor, made pro football the game it is today. I say this because it brought competition back to the game.

In the late Twenties and early Thirties, the "have" clubs, such as the Chicago Bears, the Packers, the Giants, the Redskins, and Lions stayed on top because they had the money to buy the top collegiate talent. They dominated football and whenever they played one another, they attracted big crowds.

The "have-nots"—the Steelers, the Cardinals, the Eagles, and the Dodgers—were weak, on the field and at the gate. So the rich got richer and the poor got beaten.

Although most football historians credit Bert Bell with the idea, the draft did not spring full-bloom from any one person's mind. The notion developed out of the unhealthy situation I have just described, the acute imbalance in the league; and the drive for its adoption was spearheaded by the have-not owners, firmly supported by Dick Richards.

Actually, the move for the draft had begun in 1935, about one year before the formal meeting in February, 1936, when it was finally adopted. The original aim of the draft sponsors was to break up the Bears, Redskins, Giants, and Packers. Presiding at the February meeting was Joe Carr, aided by Vice President Carl Storck. Others present were Lee Joannes and Curly Lambeau of the Packers; J. W. Mara and Steve Owen of the Giants; Halas; Bert Bell and Lud Wray of the Eagles; Marshall and Eddie Carey of the Boston Redskins; John "Shipwreck" Kelly and Dan Topping of the Dodgers; Art Rooney and Joe Bach of the Steelers; Charlie Bidwill and Arch Wolf of the Cardinals; and Richards and Potsy Clark of Detroit.

The session was stormy. Both Bell and Richards made impassioned pleas for the draft plan, arguing that it was the only way to impart balance to the league. But the opposition was stout. Halas and Mara and Lambeau and Marshall were being asked, and Richards was agreeing, to weaken their teams deliberately to benefit their rivals. Bell spoke long and argued forcefully for the draft, couching his appeal in terms of its overall advantages to the league, but his personal prestige and strategic position were not particularly high then. His franchise was one of the poorest and weakest in the league and he was vulnerable to the charge of self-seeking, in spite of his stance and words. Richards' support of the plan was critical. As one of the "haves," who stood to lose heavily if the draft was adopted, he was open to no such selfish charge. He may have been influenced originally by a desire to humble his arch rival, Halas, but would not have willingly seen his own club weakened simply to bring down the Bears. Richards had always been a strong defender of the idea of a well-balanced, competitive league.

Throughout the discussions, Halas seemed to be keeping his own counsel. Lambeau and Marshall were uncommitted; Mara unconvinced. But Halas was the key figure, not only because of his own prestige but because of the influence he exerted with Carr. When he made his move, he made it in typical Halas fashion, declaring himself unequivocally in favor of the draft because of the long-run benefits it would bring to the league. Lambeau, Marshall, and Mara then fell into line and the draft was adopted unanimously.

It was Halas, then, as it had been and would be Halas on so many earlier and later occasions, who brought his authority and influence to bear at a crucial point in the league's history, who acted decisively for the league and the league's best interests. But some of the credit must go as well to Dick Richards, whose unselfish support and defense of a plan that guaranteed the league's long success have ensured him a place among the ranks of pro football's greats.

When I began working for Richards he made it clear that I was to do more than just report the sports news. I was to make it. One sure way to make news was to get involved every summer in electing an All-Star coach. In the summer of 1937 I helped elect Gus Dorais, head coach of the University of Detroit. The choice must have been a good one. Dorais' All-Stars beat the Packers, 6-0.

Richards was trying to set up a network broadcasting of the NFL games in those days. He had a good contract with General Mills to do the Lions' games and talked them into sponsoring all NFL games on a regional basis. I helped him draw up the proposal, and we presented it at the league meeting in 1937. I explained the package to the owners. Generall Mills would pay each team $10,000 for the rights to broadcast all their home and away games, and in addition they received the rights to do the championship game. Richards and I convinced the owners to take the offer, and "Wheaties, the Breakfast of Champions" became the NFL sponsor. Jack Armstrong had joined the pros. The $10,000 per club was more than any of them were getting by themselves. In fact, some of the clubs didn't have radio coverage because they couldn't attract sponsors. We didn't have to talk too hard, and I walked around the room getting the owners' signatures on the contract. It was a good deal all around except for Richards. He had General Mills exclusively and could have kept them for himself.

When I brought the contract to Charlie Bidwill to sign he pointed to a man I didn't know who had been sitting in the back of the room and said to have him sign the contract. I gave the contract to the man, who introduced himself to me as Edward O'Hare. O'Hare was about my height, 5'9", good-looking, friendly, with an engaging personality. I liked him immediately. He looked over the contract, asked a couple of questions, and signed.

Later that evening, at the bar, I asked Bidwill who Ed O'Hare was and why he had signed the contract for him. Bidwill laughed and said, "Harry, Ed O'Hare is Big Al's lawyer and if it's OK with Ed, it's OK with Big Al! O'Hare is my lawyer too." It was obvious that "Big Al" meant Al Capone. What his relationship was to Bidwill bothered me then but I soon forgot about it. However, a few years later, I read that Ed O'Hare had been found murdered, gangland style, in Cicero. Then I remembered O'Hare from the NFL meetings, and recalled that in addition to being Capone's lawyer, he was president of Continental Wire Service, the nation's largest bookmaking wire operation. O'Hare's son, Butch, was killed during World War II.

Butch was a graduate of the United States Naval Academy and was an ace pilot in the Pacific before he met his death. O'Hare Field in Chicago was named in his honor.

On Christmas Eve, 1937, Harry Kipke, the football coach at Michigan, was fired. However, his overall record had been excellent, and he was also one of the Wolverines' all-time athletic greats. A heated controversy developed over Kipke's dismissal and the press and radio had a field day editorializing over the incident. The situation seemed tailormade. Kipke was a natural candidate for All-Star coach. His record was good enough, and he would benefit from all the publicity. I called Kipke, who had taken a job at Ford, and he agreed, provided his employer would approve. His boss was Harry Bennett, chief assistant to Henry Ford, Sr. Next to the senior Ford, Bennett was probably the most influential man in the Ford organization.

Kipke set up a meeting between Bennett and me, and I told Bennett of my plans. He thought it was a good idea for Kipke to run and gave his approval. Bennett told me he wanted Kipke to run for regent of the University of Michigan and he figured the publicity would be good for his man. In Michigan the regents are elected like the governor or legislature, and Bennett wanted Kipke elected so he could fire the coaches and dictate athletic policy. If Kipke won the All-Star job it would prove very embarrassing to the people at Michigan who fired him and to the Big Ten as well. I explained that to Bennett, who couldn't have cared less.

To get the campaign launched, Bennett set up a luncheon at the Recess Club in the Fisher Building. He had the top manufacturers' agents who dealt with Ford there and I explained the operation to them. Bennett took contributions from them and set up a fund of about $100,000 for me to use. No one questioned Bennett when he told them how much to give. I drew on that fund for operating expenses and accounted to Bennett.

When the scope of the Kipke campaign became apparent to

Arch Ward and the *Chicago Tribune* people, they asked me to
call off the drive. Even though the publicity was good for the
Tribune, the Big Ten had threatened to pull out of the All-Star
game if Kipke was elected. Ward was in a real bind and knew
it. The Big Ten insisted that Alvin "Bo" McMillin be elected.
Bennett was just as determined that Kipke take down the
honors, and since we had the votes, we thought we couldn't
lose. We were sending thousands of votes every day to Ward,
and finally Wilfred Smith, then Ward's assistant, came to
Detroit complaining that Kipke now had more votes than
Roosevelt received when he won the 1936 Presidential race.

Since Ford dealers and parts manufacturers all over the world
had been backing Kipke, Smith was probably right. He repeated
what we already knew, that the *Tribune* could not let Kipke in,
and a few days later the paper declared McMillin the winner,
with Kipke second. Bennett didn't fret about the results because
Kipke received so much publicity during the campaign that he
was a cinch to win the regents seat in November, which he did.
The *Tribune,* meanwhile, determined to avoid any future
squeezes, eliminated the voting method and thereafter ap-
pointed the coach. When all the furor was settled, the *Tribune*
still had the Big Ten's support, Harry Bennett had his regent,
and I had won Bennett's valued friendship.

Meanwhile, my radio career prospered, but in 1938 Richards'
Lions had begun to slip. Richards himself was sick and had
moved from Detroit to his ranch outside Palm Springs, California. I was virtually running the club until Richards hired
"Gloomy Gus" Henderson, former coach at the University of
Southern California, to be the Lions' coach and he took over the
team. At that time I didn't see anything wrong with my handling the team and also broadcasting the Lions games but I
could hardly have been an objective reporter. My first responsibility was to Richards, not the fans of Detroit. Under Henderson, the Lions continued to slip, and by the end of the 1939

season they were near the bottom of the league. If anything was to be salvaged from the season, it had to be in the draft, and Richards had come up with a pretty fair draft prospect—Clyde "Bulldog" Turner of Hardin-Simmons in Texas.

Richards had seen Turner play on the Coast, took a liking to him, and told Turner the Lions wanted him. Richards, however, knew that other clubs in the league also were interested in Turner, especially the Bears, so Richards dashed off to Abilene, Turner's home town, and told Bulldog to tell everyone who asked that he wasn't interested in playing pro football. Turner's teeth were in bad shape so Richards gave him $200 to get them fixed.

Then Richards called Henderson and me and told us to choose Turner, if possible, as our first choice. Since other clubs had talked to Turner and he had faithfully told them he wouldn't play pro ball, we figured we had a lock on him. Sure enough, as the draft began at the Schroeder Hotel in Milwaukee, the teams drafting ahead of us passed over Turner. When it came Detroit's turn to pick, Gloomy Gus bellowed out, "Doyle Nave of USC." Halas then claimed Turner, who became the all-time, all-pro center for the Bears. Nave never even made the Lions exhibition team that next season.

I had been in the Press room, but as soon as I heard the news I called Richards to tell him what had happened. He told me to put the club up for sale. If he couldn't have his instructions followed, then he wanted out. I told Carr and Halas of Richards' decision and released the news to the press. Of course, Richards also fired Henderson. But Gloomy Gus had an ace up his sleeve. He had saved some letters that Richards had written him during the season, and the night before the draft, figuring Richards would let him go for not following instructions, he turned the letters over to Halas.

Everyone knew Richards gambled, as did many of the other owners. They always bet on their own team, and in those days odds, not points, were used to indicate the differences between teams. In the letters he had foolishly written to Henderson, Richards revealed that he had bet heavily on a number of the Lions' games and called for everyone's best efforts to win for him.

Then, as now, it was against the league charter for an owner or player or coach to bet. The rule wasn't enforced but the owners were careful not to put anything in writing. Richards had violated that unwritten covenant and Henderson saw his chance to embarrass Richards and the league by releasing the letters to Halas.

Halas called me to discuss the matter, and he agreed nothing would be gained by releasing the story to the press, and in Richards' condition, the notoriety might kill him. Halas kept the secret of Richards' betting for years and it only became public knowledge in December of 1964.

The mystery of why Henderson picked Doyle Nave still puzzles me. Certainly the USC tie wasn't that binding. Henderson knew he would be fired by Richards for not picking Turner. Perhaps he felt the letters he had would intimidate Richards and enable him to keep his job. But why flaunt his instructions in the first place? If the league and Halas actually had possession of Richards' letters before the draft, then the Turner incident was a perfect ploy for Richards to use to bow out gracefully and spare the league the embarrassment of asking for his resignation. I'm sure that whatever the decision on handling the problem, Halas and Richards worked it out between themselves and only Halas knows the real facts. In any event, the league had been shielded by Halas from the damaging publicity and public confidence in pro football was preserved.

Thus ended the colorful career of Dick Richards in pro football. At Palm Springs, Richards kept a mock graveyard on his property with small headstones for each of his colleagues in the NFL. His arch rival George Halas was there, along with

Mara, Marshall, and Lambeau. Now he could add a stone for
Gloomy Gus Henderson and one for the Lions.

Although I had now become well-known in the Midwest as a
sports broadcaster I wanted to move to New York, where the
money and power was in almost all businesses, but particularly
in broadcasting and communications. In 1941 I auditioned,
along with many other people, for Graham McNamee's job on
the old Blue network of NBC. I got the job. Almost immediately, Bill Stern and Ted Husing contacted me. Stern was sports
director for the Red network of NBC, and Husing, for CBS.
We met at Toots Shor's and after reminiscing a bit with Stern,
they both got around to the real business at hand—advising me
not to undercut their price for doing a football game. They got
$1500. I told them they had nothing to worry about, that my
asking price would be $2500. They laughed at me, but I got the
$2500 per game and soon Stern and Husing had raised their
price to mine.

New York was a year-round festival. I was doing just about
every major sporting event in the country, with special empha-
sis on Notre Dame football and the NFL on Sundays. Stern and
I worked out a schedule whereby we would split the major
games each Saturday, Bill taking one and I the other. I always
made sure that at least half my coverage included Notre
Dame games, for with the Notre Dame games went the highest
ratings.

In 1942, with the country at war, I took an apartment in
Washington, D.C. and began broadcasting the Redskin games.
Several years before, George Marshall had asked me to broad-
cast for him but I had been reluctant to leave Richards and
Detroit and had declined. Now I took Marshall up on his offer.
Washington was the seat of power and influence in the nation,
and I wanted to be part of it. I now had an apartment in New

York, one in Washington, and my home in Dearborn, Michigan. During the week I worked for Harry Bennett and Henry Ford at Willow Run as their Public Relations Director, and on weekends I'd travel the country doing a big college game on Saturday and the Redskins on Sunday.

Because of my position, I became intimate with the power elite in Washington, and during the course of my broadcasts I would mention many of the people I had met and come to know well in official Washington. Shirley Povich and Bob Addie, the fine writers for the *Washington Post,* used to kid me about mentioning that people were at the games when actually they were not within twenty miles of the stadium. Sometimes they were right. I recall a time when Lou Nichols, personnel director for J. Edgar Hoover and the FBI, was recuperating at home after an operation and I called him to inquire about his health. The next day the Redskins played, and the weather was foul. During my broadcast, I told the radio audience that Senator Smathers and Senator Symington and J. Edgar Hoover were taking in the game. Then—"And there is my good friend, Lou Nichols of the FBI. It's nice to see him up and around after his operation." That night Hoover called Nichols and dressed him down for being out at the game in such vile weather. Nichols asked Hoover if he had enjoyed the game and when Hoover denied being there, Nichols also said he had not set foot inside the stadium, but that Harry Wismer had both of them in the stands, enjoying the game immensely. Both kidded me for years about the incident. I've often been asked why I always mention famous people who are in attendance at games. It's simple—it lends glamor to the event, the fans like to hear who's there, and the person concerned enjoys the publicity. If occasionally I happen to mention someone who doesn't happen to be there, no one is hurt and that person still enjoys the plug.

J. Edgar Hoover and I became great friends and many times I would join him at his home for dinner. One evening I was with him when he had Sir Winston Churchill as his dinner guest. He and Hoover discussed the status of bookmakers in their respective countries. In England a bookmaker was recognized as a legitimate businessman, Sir Winston said, and often achieved high social position. Some of Britain's most distinguished persons, he went on, had been bookmakers. Churchill kidded Hoover about the position of bookmakers in the States. Hoover, who finds betting at the track one of his favorite forms of relaxation, was hard put to justify our laws on bookmaking, since there was really no sensible answer. The two biggest gambling houses in the world are the New York Stock Exchange and the American Stock Exchange. And if speculating on stock isn't gambling, then I don't know what you would call it.

In 1946, Hoover nominated me for one of the ten outstanding young men to be selected by the U.S. Junior Chamber of Commerce. I tied for first place with a young Congressman from Massachusetts, John F. Kennedy. I met Kennedy for the first time at the awards dinner in Chicago in 1947 and we became good friends. Over the years the future President and I would get together at Burning Tree Country Club in Washington; and in 1959 and '60, when his eyes were fixed solidly on the Presidency, he would attend football games and at halftime be interviewed over radio and television. This was great exposure for him and certainly helped make his face familiar across the nation.

My official association with George Preston Marshall and the Washington Redskins began in 1942, when I went to Washington and began broadcasting their games. But I had first met Marshall at the NFL meetings in 1935. Marshall, along with Halas, dominated the league. He is a most complex person and anyone who one day thinks he knows the real George, finds himself facing a new George the next time they meet. He loved football and probably expressed it best when he would meet me at halftime during the game and talk to the radio listeners.

His constant theme was that football was for the rugged, and that its success was due to the fact that it typified the tough, aggressive nature of the American people. As he would state it: "Football is no place for soft people."

Marshall did a great deal for the NFL and helped teams that were floundering by deliberately passing top-notch talent to them. He shipped Frank Filchock and Charlie Conerly to the New York Giants when Mara's team needed help in the Forties Of course, these two fine passers were expendable to Marshall because he had Sammy Baugh, but he could have kept them or driven much harder bargains for them. George had learned what Richards, Halas, and Bell had passionately preached— keep the league balanced; bolster the weak clubs; above all, do not let the New York franchise flounder.

When I first started as the 'Skins' announcer, Marshall had a local beer sponsor and the games were carried on a tiny 250-watt station. Through Harry Bennett, the American Oil Company became my sponsor and with their backing I developed the first radio network for an NFL team. Amoco and the director of their Baltimore ad agency, Joseph Katz, helped me widen the broadcast area of the Redskins to include all of the South and much of the mid-Atlantic states. Soon Marshall had the largest single-area coverage of any NFL team and his profits from broadcasting increased considerably.

Marshall hired and fired more coaches than any owner in football. He was forever second-guessing his coach and sometimes would actually do the substituting. Only two, Ray (Red) Flaherty and Joe Kuharich, really had George's confidence. With Flaherty, the 'Skins won five division titles and two world championships.

Marshall's team won the Eastern Division title in 1945 and we travelled to Cleveland to play Dan Reeves' Cleveland Rams for the title, I to do the broadcast. The weather was frightful —the temperature hovered around zero—and George's pet, the

Redskin band, couldn't perform because the lips of the men in the brass section froze to the mouthpiece of their instruments. Guiding the Rams was Bob Waterfield, a rookie quarterback who already had shown signs of greatness. The key to the 'Skins' offense was the incomparable Baugh. The wind was blowing in gusts up to 50 or 60 miles per hour, and late in the first quarter Baugh faded into the end zone to pass. He threw, but the wind blew the ball against the crossbar and it fell into the end zone.

I didn't know what to call it. But George Halas, sitting with me in the radio coop, whispered "safety" and that's how I interpreted the play for the radio listeners. The officials, players, and coaches seemed to be as confused as I had been; but finally one official, with the rule book out, signaled a safety. The Rams beat the 'Skins, 15-14, and the safety was the difference. Marshall was furious at the loss. We were in the hotel lobby after the game when Dick DeGroot, the 'Skins' coach, walked in. DeGroot walked up to us and said, "A terrible thing happened to us today." Marshall snapped, "Don't tell me—I was there and I know all about it!" DeGroot looked at George in surprise and said, "You knew my wife lost her purse at the game?" "You're fired!" roared Marshall.

DeGroot was gone and at the next league meeting, the rule was changed to read that if a pass, thrown from the end zone, struck the crossbar and bounded back into the end zone, it would be ruled merely an incomplete pass. Only Halas, of all the owners, would have known that the rule was in the books, and I was lucky enough to have him as my guest during the game.

Marshall had Baugh. That meant he could have any coach he wanted because with Sammy, the 'Skins were sure to be in the thick of things for the title. With the possible exception of Walter Johnson, Baugh was the most popular athlete in Washington history. He was also the best passer who ever lived. The stories about Baugh's amazing feats are countless and need no recounting from me. Suffice to say, I found him to be the most exciting player I ever saw, and I saw a lot of him and many others. I was in the booth when Sam appeared with the College All-Stars against the Green Bay Packers in 1937; and beginning in 1942, I broadcast every game he played in until his retirement. If he were playing today, his would be the greatest name in all sports.

Sam was quiet and reserved and never drank, although he did chew tobacco, even during a game, and enjoyed cigars. Sam's personal life was above reproach, and the only time his off-the-field activities created headlines was in 1943 when the Washington *Times-Herald* printed a story that Sam was gambling and that he and other Redskins had pulled off some betting coups. One of Sam's friends was reputed to be a local bookmaker, and Sam frequently was seen with him in public. The stories never ruffled Sam; the man was his friend—that was that. When the story broke, Elmer Layden, NFL commissioner, announced that he personally would go to Washington and investigate. He needn't have bothered. Marshall rounded up his team, and he and Baugh marched them into the managing editor's office at the *Times-Herald*. "Point out the gamblers if your story is true," bellowed Marshall. "Produce the facts or retract your story." The editor took one frightened look at Marshall and the roomful of players, swallowed, and shook his head. He had no facts. Marshall and the team left. The paper retracted its story.

PART II

THE BLIND WAR

Joe Carr died on May 20, 1939. After the proper mourning period, the NFL met to select a new commissioner for the league. George Halas made the first selection—Arch Ward, sports editor of the *Chicago Tribune*. If Ward had accepted there probably would not have been any All America Football Conference nor any American Football League today. But Ward turned Halas down and recommended Elmer Layden, one of the Four Horsemen of Notre Dame, for the job. Halas concurred, Layden accepted, and the league ratified.

During the latter stages of World War II, a number of people tried to get new franchises in the National Football League, only to be turned down. Arch Ward, after turning down the NFL in 1939, decided in 1944 that there was room for another league. Like Ban Johnson, who thirty-five years earlier had established the American League to challenge the National League in baseball, Ward organized a league to compete with the now solidly entrenched NFL. Ward had two big advantages going for him—the obvious interest in pro football in cities where there wasn't an NFL franchise and World War II. The war had unsettled pro football, as it had every other facet of American life. When they returned home, players were re-

33

ceptive to the idea of two leagues bidding for their services, and if the clubs that wanted them were near the area where they wanted to live, so much the better. The NFL had a hard time convincing veterans of Anzio, Iwo Jima, and Bastogne that they had to return to the club that originally owned them.

Before World War II there had been a number of abortive efforts to form a league to rival the NFL. But the All America Football Conference had Arch Ward, probably the greatest of all sports promoters, as its master architect. From Ward's fertile brain sprang the All-Star baseball game, the All-Star football game, the Golden Gloves, the Silver Skates, and many other famous sporting events that are still staged today. Literally hundreds of millions of dollars have been raised for charity through the sporting events originated by Arch Ward in conjunction with the *Chicago Tribune* Charities, Inc. It is interesting that Don Maxwell, managing editor of the *Chicago Tribune,* George Halas, and Arch Ward were the closest of friends; and one wonders what must have gone through Maxwell's mind when his good friend and sports editor, one of the best-known sports figures in the nation, began organizing a league to compete against the league that was built and developed by another of his closest friends, George Halas.

Ward began to organize the All America Football Conference two years before its formal debut in 1946. There was no secret about the move, but the National Football League refused to pay any attention to it. In fact, Elmer Layden dismissed the entire enterprise with the comment, "Let them get a football and play a game and then we will see how good they are." Layden's disregard for the new conference was to have disastrous effects, since Dan Topping, owner of the Brooklyn franchise in the NFL, jumped to the AAFC in 1946. Topping wanted to move his NFL team from tiny Ebbets Field into Yankee Stadium; and he dickered with Tim Mara of the New York Giants, still playing in the Polo Grounds, for playing dates that would satisfy both Mara and himself. If Topping had been permitted to go into Yankee Stadium and work out favorable schedules with Mara, it is highly unlikely that the AAFC would have ever gotten off the ground. Without a New York franchise, a major sport cannot survive. Layden should have acted but he ignored Topping's pleas for assistance, and when the All America Football Conference was formed, Topping joined it, got Yankee Stadium for his team, and left the NFL.

In 1946 the All America Football Conference was made up of eight teams—the Cleveland Browns, the Buffalo Bills, the Brooklyn Dodgers, the Miami Seahawks, the San Francisco '49ers, the Los Angeles Dons, the Chicago Rockets, and Topping's New York Yankees. Arthur B. McBride, successful in the taxicab business and the newspaper field, was the owner of the Cleveland Browns. McBride also was president of the Continental Wire Service, Ed O'Hare's late position. The Buffalo team was owned by James F. Breuil, a wealthy oilman from Oklahoma City, Oklahoma, who held the Buffalo franchise because Buffalo was the only city available. He had tried to join the NFL and had been refused. William D. Cox, a lumber man who also owned the Philadelphia Phillies baseball team, owned the Brooklyn franchise for one year, but it was then taken over by the Brooklyn Dodgers baseball company, headed by Branch Rickey. The Miami Seahawks under Harvey Hester, a genial, gracious man, survived only one year in that winter paradise and then were moved to Baltimore as the original Baltimore Colts. The San Francisco '49ers were the realization of a dream of two brothers in the lumber-trucking business, Victor P. Morabito and his brother, Anthony J. The Morabitos had tried to join the NFL in the early Forties and also had been turned down. They were rejected for a number of reasons, but in particular because George Preston Marshall said that he would quit the league if he were ever faced with the necessity of having to pay travel expenses to the West Coast. A few years later,

Dan Reeves, owner of the Cleveland Rams, moved his team to
Los Angeles and, although Marshall also was opposed to this
move, Reeves threatened to jump to the AAFC unless the NFL
approved the shift. Marshall, however, insisted that Reeves pay
the difference in travel costs for teams travelling from Chicago
to the coast and Reeves agreed. The approval by the NFL of
the Reeves move, although given under duress, proved to be
an unmixed blessing for the NFL. In time the Los Angeles
operation would develop into one of the most successful and
profitable in NFL history.

Had Reeves not decided to go to Los Angeles and had he not
forced the NFL's approval, the All America Football Conference, with the Dons and '49ers, would have had the California
gold mine all to itself. As it was, Ben Lindheimer's Dons out-
drew the Rams and Bob Waterfield in the Los Angeles Coliseum during their first two years of head-to-head competition.
Certainly the rivalry with the San Francisco '49ers had a great
deal to do with the success of the Dons in the mid-Forties. The
two leagues themselves, however, met head on in only three
cities. One was in Los Angeles. They also vied in New York, but
in the big town the NFL had the established New York Giants
in the Polo Grounds facing the young New York Yankees in
Yankee Stadium and the Brooklyn Dodgers in Ebbets Field.
The Giants in the late Forties were no worldbeaters, but they
soon revived when a young quarterback from the University of
Mississippi named Charlie Conerly arrived at the Polo Grounds
by way of Washington. Conerly, whom George Marshall had
passed along to the Giants "to keep the New York franchise
strong," soon would lead the Giants from their dog days of the
Forties to their glory days of the Fifties and early Sixties. The
third city where the two leagues met head-to-head was Chicago. There the Bears of George Halas and the Cardinals of
Charlie Bidwill had been established for years. Though the

Bears always had the best of it in both field and gate competition, Bidwill's Cardinals of '47 and '48 became one of the powerhouses of the NFL. The Rockets of the AAFC had the strong support of the *Chicago Tribune* in trying to lure fans into mammoth Soldier Field and, in addition, boasted three of the greatest players in Big Ten history: Elroy "Crazylegs" Hirsch, who later became one of football's immortals with the Los Angeles Rams; Bob Hoernschmeyer from Indiana, who later became one of the stalwarts of the great Detroit Lions teams of the Fifties; and Billy Hillenbrand, also of Indiana. Piloting this trio was famed Angelo Bertelli, the Heisman Trophy winner and star Notre Dame quarterback of the early Forties.

To compete against this glamorous collection of midwestern stars, Halas came up with a surefire weapon—a championship team in 1946, the feared and famed Monsters of the Midway—Luckman, McAfee, Osmanski, Fortmann, Stydahar, *et al*. Then the Cardinals, who in 1945 had won only one game, in 1946 under Jimmy Conzelman moved up to a 6 and 5 record. In 1947 the Eagles and Cardinals met for the championship and Bidwill's dream backfield—Pat Harder from Wisconsin, Elmer Angsman from Notre Dame, Charlie Trippi from Georgia, and Paul Christman from Missouri—moved the championship to Chicago's South Side, beating the Eagles 28-21.

Had the AAFC been able to compete with the NFL in Chicago as they were able to compete in Los Angeles and to a lesser extent in New York, the new league might have succeeded. But Halas and Bidwill, whether by chance, though probably through shrewd planning, came up with successive championship teams to take the play away from the Rockets.

But if the AAFC was losing out in Chicago, it had a winner in Cleveland. Under a gridiron genius, Paul Brown, the Cleveland Browns became a superteam. Brown had never coached in pro football until he was signed in 1944 by Mickey McBride,

Browns' owner, to coach the Browns of the new All-America Football Conference. Brown had had a successful career at Massillon High School in Ohio where his teams won 58 of 60 games, and later moved to Ohio State University where his 1942 team won the national championship. In 1943 he joined the Navy as a Lieutenant Commander and coached the Great Lakes football team which defeated Notre Dame two years in a row. It was while at Great Lakes that Brown first saw Marion Motley in action. Motley had been a high school star in Ohio when Brown was the coach at Massillon, although he had never played against a Brown-coached team.

I mentioned that Brown was hired by Mickey McBride in 1944. McBride gave Brown $1,000 a month from 1944 until Brown was discharged from the service in 1945. The team that Brown put together was named after him, and it contributed many brilliant stars to the pro game—Otto Graham, Motley, Lou Groza, Bill Willis, Lou Rymkus, Len Ford, Mac Speedie, and Dante Lavelli. The Browns' record in the All-America Football Conference for the four years of its existence shows a staggering 52 wins, 4 losses, and 3 ties.

Another premier team of the AAFC was the San Francisco '49ers. Led by their great coach Buck Shaw, the '49ers boasted such standouts as Frankie Albert, Joe "The Jet" Perry, Bruno Banducci, and the former Bear great Norm Standlee. In addition to these stars at San Francisco and Cleveland, there were such players in the AAFC as Glenn Dobbs, a Tulsa great playing for the Brooklyn Dodgers; Dobbs' teammate Martin Ruby; George Ratterman of the Buffalo Bills; and Claude "Buddy" Young, Spec Sanders, Arnie Weinmeister, and Otto Schnellbacher of the New York Yankees. In 1948 a balding young quarterback by the name of Yelberton Abraham Tittle joined a new team, the Baltimore Colts. As a whole, the quality of the players in the All-America Football Conference was not much below that of the National Football League. Mainly because they had at least one-third of their roster seasoned with pro veterans, plus a great deal of talented youngsters, the AAFC clubs could have given the NFL clubs an argument anywhere, anytime.

But if the AAFC had great stars, so did the NFL; and as the rivalry between the two leagues mounted, adherents of each side kept the fires of the Hot Stove League burning brightly. The NFL boasted such great old-timers as Baugh, Luckman, Turner, the dream backfield of the Cardinals, and the great Eagle teams of the Forties with Steve Van Buren, Pete Pihos, Bucko Kilroy, and Chuck Bednarik. On the Coast were the wonder quarterbacks Bob Waterfield and Norm Van Brocklin throwing to Tom Fears and Glenn Davis, the former "Mr. Outside" of Army.

If the two leagues were relatively equal in playing personnel, they were also equal in one other important factor—the ability to lose money. The war was costing both leagues a tremendous amount of money, and the cost of signing new players became more and more prohibitive each year. If there was one single benefit to come out of the war between the two leagues it was the skyrocketing price for talent which accrued to the players. The asking price for linemen and backs jumped two and three times to what it had been before World War II and it never again fell below that level. Other major beneficiaries were the fans of the AAFC clubs, many of whom had never before seen football as the pros played it.

But it takes money—money that comes from gate receipts— to run a pro football club. There was no television of pro football in those days, nobody to underwrite the cost of these teams as there is today. And if it takes money to run a pro football team, only a few clubs in either league were drawing enough

people in the late Forties to pay the salaries the players demanded. Take a look at the champion Philadelphia Eagles of
'48 and '49. They were sold to a syndicate in 1949 because
Alexis Thompson, owner of the Eagles, couldn't stand the losses
he was suffering. He had one of the finest teams in the history
of the NFL, and yet the Eagles weren't drawing enough fans to
tiny Shibe Park to meet the payroll.

The Pittsburgh Steelers were saved only because the popular
Jock Sutherland coached the Steelers before capacity crowds in
1946 and 1947. In Los Angeles, Dan Reeves had to give up
two-thirds of his franchise to wealthy men in the Hollywood
area who agreed to assume a share of his losses. The Giants'
franchise sagged badly for years during the pro war. Ted Collins, who owned the Boston franchise in the NFL and later
moved to New York, had to give up in 1951 after two years
in New York. He estimated his losses at between $900,000 and
$1 million. I know that George Marshall had felt the pressure
of the war, because I bought 25 percent of the Redskins early
in 1950. Marshall needed the money to continue operating.

Only the Bears and the Cards escaped the heat, since each
came up with a championship team in '46 and '47, respectively,
and the fierce rivalry between the two teams helped their gate
receipts. But in Detroit the Lions were sold at a loss in a transaction which brought me my first part-ownership of a NFL
franchise.

In the All America Football Conference, Miami failed after
one year and Baltimore entered the league. Even with the bril-
liant young Y. A. Tittle, the Baltimore franchise staggered.
Brooklyn quit after three years, even before the AAFC folded,
and joined the New York Yankees of Dan Topping in a seven-
club league in 1949. The Cleveland Browns, the stellar AAFC
attraction, drew 60,135 people into mammoth Municipal
Stadium in Cleveland for their first league game. Until that

time, that was one of the largest crowds in the history of the game. Yet, four years later, when they played the San Francisco '49ers for the championship of the AAFC, less than 20,000 people watched from the stands. The payoff to the winning Browns in 1949 was about $275 per man, and to the losing '49ers, about $170, mere chickenfeed.

To my way of thinking, two factors contributed to the death of the AAFC. First, there was no public outlet for the games, i.e., television; and second, the AAFC had no balance. The greatest strength of the AAFC lay in the Cleveland Browns. Yet the Browns were so superior to the rest of the league that the Cleveland fans soon became blasé and stopped supporting the team. The AAFC would never be vindicated until the league had folded and the Browns met the Philadelphia Eagles, champions of the NFL, in the first game of the now-merged leagues in 1950. On that September evening over 75,000 came to Municipal Stadium in Philadelphia to watch. The Browns made believers of them all as they beat the defending world-champion Eagles, 35-10, with Bert Bell and most of the other NFL owners looking on.

My good friend Arch Ward told me in 1947 that Fred Mandel, owner of the Lions, was anxious to sell the club to avoid any more losses. I saw Mandel in Chicago about a week later and he confirmed that he wanted to sell. His asking price was $165,000, or about $60,000 less than the amount he had paid for the club in 1939. Mandel added that he, being a Chicagoan, felt uncomfortable owning a Detroit franchise, particularly since the All America Football Conference had been working on Chicago businessmen to support the Rockets of the new league. Arch Ward and Dan Topping had been making a strong pitch to Edwin Anderson to form an All America Football Conference syndicate in Detroit and chal-

lenge the Lions. I returned to Detroit after seeing Mandel
and went golfing at Bloomfield Hills Country Club with
Lyall Fife, Walter "Spike" Briggs, Jr., and Charles T. Fisher.
Jr. Soon Phil Downey, Charles Hoffman, and Anderson
came in; and the seven of us, who had come together by
chance, remained together and started talking about football. Knowing that Mandel was interested in selling and that
Ward had made a pitch to Anderson to start an AAFC franchise
in Detroit, I mentioned that it would be a good idea for Michigan people to take over the ownership of the pro football franchise in Detroit. At that time the Detroit Red Wings in the
National Hockey League were owned by Jim Norris of Chicago,
and Mandel, of course, owned the Lions. Only the Detroit
Tigers were owned locally, by Briggs, Jr.'s father. Everyone
agreed that it was a good idea and after talking it over we
decided to have a few more meetings to see what the possibilities were. Since I had made the initial contact with Mandel, it
was up to me to handle the negotiations, and finally everyone
agreed that Mandel's asking price was reasonable. We each put
up $20,000 and Fisher arranged a loan of $25,000 through the
National Bank of Detroit. The bank didn't require any collateral, since Fisher was the bank's president. I knew the other
six quite well, but Briggs and Fife had been close friends of
mine for about ten years. I had first met them at the Fox
Theater in Detroit, where I also first met Ed Sullivan. Sullivan,
now the director of the popular Ed Sullivan Show on CBS-TV,
was an emcee at the Fox Theater. Years later I got him what I
think was his first major sponsorship through the Ford Motor
Company. When news of our negotiations broke, I got a call
from Richards in Palm Springs.

Richards was still incapacitated from his heart attack, but he
couldn't forget what had happened to him in the NFL and,
friendship notwithstanding, he threatened me with loss of my

outlets on his radio stations if I joined the syndicate to purchase
the Lions. Richards had done a lot for me, and I wanted to
spare him any additional pain and worry, but I desperately
wanted to join the franchise. Spike Briggs, whose father re-
garded all pro football players as "Sunday afternoon wrestlers,"
was confronted with a similar problem. His father warned him
to get out of the syndicate and Spike was beginning to waver.
With both of us over a barrel, it looked as if the syndicate
would fold; but Spike and I, after a long meeting, decided to
continue. We believed that the Lions were a worthwhile invest-
ment and that we shouldn't permit outside pressures to sway
us. But we couldn't bring Richards and Briggs, Sr., around to
our way of thinking nor could we afford to test the strength of
their threats, so we made arrangements to place our stock in
the franchise in the names of other people. I chose my father-
in-law, Roy Bryant, to be my assignee. Roy is the brother of
Mrs. Clara Ford, the wife of the senior Henry. Conrad Knowle,
Jr., of Springfield, Illinois, drew up the contract for me. The
contract stipulated that Bryant would be protected while he
held the stock but could not sell the shares to anyone but me.
I would assume any obligations if the company lost money and
I would make up the difference if the stock were ultimately
sold below the $20,000 original cost. If there were any suit
against the Lions, I, and not Bryant, would be liable. Bryant
had no right to sell my stock, and this was why he was the only
one to vote against the sale of the franchise to William Clay
Ford in January of 1964. Spike Briggs, Jr., made a similar arrangement. Devious? Perhaps it was, but we felt the means
justified in view of the unreasonable pressures being exerted
against us. And I dare say that there are many businesses in this
country and many sports franchises with silent owners.

In 1950, at George Marshall's request, I bought into the
Redskins. I had been doing their games for a number of years

and had been closely involved in the NFL. Marshall phoned me in Detroit one day saying that he had had an argument with Leo DeOrsey and that DeOrsey was out of the Redskin organization. If I wanted to buy DeOrsey's stock, I could buy six shares for $14,000. The six shares represented 6 percent of the club. DeOrsey was a lawyer who had been in and out of the Redskin organization and had had frequent run-ins with Marshall. A few days later, Marshall called me back and asked if I would like to buy another fourteen shares for $30,000, all in all, 25 percent of the Redskin stock, which I did. Now I owned one-seventh of the Detroit Lions and one-fourth of the Washington Redskins. It had been assumed for years that no one could be complete or part owner of more than one ball club in the National Football League. I was part owner of two clubs. In my suit to recover my stock from my ex-father-in-law in 1964, Wilbur Brucker, former Secretary of the Army under Eisenhower, and lawyer for Bryant, said that in the history of the NFL no one had ever owned shares in more than one club. Lyall Fife, a co-owner with me in the Lions, testified that as late as 1955 he knew that Charlie Bidwill, owner of the Chicago Cardinals, also held an interest in the Chicago Bears, supposedly owned outright by George Halas. That was the end of Bryant's case. I recovered the $100,000 due me for the shares I owned in the Lions in December, 1964.

It was apparent to insiders that after the 1948 season the All America Football Conference was going under. The weaknesses of certain franchises were quite apparent and the NFL owners began to breathe more easily. Though rumors of a merger between the two leagues had been prevalent since the beginning of the AAFC, it wasn't until January of 1949 that the AAFC owners met with the NFL owners and Bert Bell in Philadelphia. The AAFC was dying but it had to be permitted a graceful death. Because the owners had commitments to one another and to the cities in which their franchises were located, they were unable to close their books in '48 and were forced to meet their obligations through the '49 season. Bert Bell did everything in his power to make the demise of the AAFC as palatable as possible. But there were many legal as well as emotional problems, and the negotiations stretched on for months. Rumors of these negotiations undoubtedly cut into gate receipts for both leagues in 1949. Finally, the AAFC owners agreed to merge if the NFL would accept Baltimore as well as Cleveland and San Francisco in the National Football League. The NFL, the year before, had balked against accepting Baltimore, but after a year of negotiating between Bell and the AAFC, after a debilitating war and depleted wallets, the NFL finally admitted Baltimore.

There was one very ticklish problem that still had to be solved, and that was the disposition of the players who would be cut loose when the remaining five AAFC franchises folded. There was an unexpected flare-up at the NFL meeting in January of 1950 when Mickey McBride threatened to take his Browns out of football because he wasn't going to be permitted to take in Jim Breiul, Buffalo owner, as a 25 percent partner and claim six players from the Bills roster. The NFL owners refused to consent to the arrangement, and Bell was finally able to soothe McBride's feelings and to make a compromise that allotted three of the Bills to Cleveland.

The New York situation was somewhat complicated. Suffice to say that there were three teams in the New York area in 1949. The New York Yankees of the AAFC, the already established New York Giants of Tim Mara, and the New York Yanks, a team that had transferred in the NFL from Boston to New York to play in the Polo Grounds. Ted Collins moved to New York from Boston in 1949 and renamed his team the New York Bulldogs. Because Topping, owner of the AAFC New

York Yanks, and of the New York Yankee baseball team and
Yankee Stadium, and Horace Stoneham, owner of the Polo
Grounds, who had the Giants as tenants, quarreled over where
Collins' team would play, the merger was held up. Collins had
signed a lease with Stoneham for ten years when he moved his
Boston franchise to New York. Stoneham wasn't going to permit
Collins to transfer to the Yankee Stadium because two teams
playing in Yankee Stadium might prove formidable to the
Giants in the Polo Grounds, and Yankee Stadium offered a far
more attractive place to play than the old stadium under
Coogan's Bluff.

The key person in the transaction was Buddy Young, and
Topping argued that it would cripple his Yankees if Buddy
Young were passed over to the Giants. Bell agreed and said that
Young should play for the Yankees. When Collins became unreasonable about the way Bell was proceeding and balked at
making concessions to Stoneham, whose lease he had signed,
Bell decided to make the choices for Collins' club. The Giants
and Yankees picked one-two for the first six rounds, and the
players who remained then were assigned to Collins' new team.

After two years in Yankee Stadium, Collins' team transferred to Dallas and in 1952 became the Dallas Texans. They
limped along in Dallas for about half the season, by which
time it had become obvious that the Texans' appetites had
not yet sweetened to pro football; and for the rest of the season the transplanted New Yorkers played on the road. At one
time, in November 1952, they met the Bears in Akron, Ohio,
and drew only 3,000 people.

The war was over. The All America Football Conference,
many of whose players would now augment the NFL ranks,
could have competed on fairly even terms with their older
rivals on the field. If television had been on the scene in 1945,
as it is today, there is no doubt that the All America Football

Conference would have survived. Its teams played exciting football, had some of the top players in the game, and some of the great coaches. The war had been costly to both leagues; but as the Fifties began, the leagues had merged and one man commanded the center of the stage—Bert Bell.

PART III

THE FABULOUS FIFTIES

The NFL was now truly national. From New York to Los Angeles, pro football began crowding baseball as America's number one professional sport. In the Thirties and Forties the owners had had the final say in league matters. But with the advent of television, with the league expanding, and with public interest in the game mounting, pro football needed a strong, decisive commissioner to direct its operation. He was already in office—Bert Bell.

It was obvious toward the end of 1945 that Elmer Layden was on the way out. The owners were not satisfied with the way he was handling the AAFC (the new league would be in full operation in 1946) and Layden was Arch Ward's man. With Halas and Ward feuding, and with Ward being the man who had put together the AAFC, Layden's position couldn't have been shakier. The owners met in January of 1946 to dismiss Layden, but before Halas could wield the ax, Tim Mara spoke: "I am not going to vote for anybody until this group votes Layden a year's pay with our thanks." So spoke the owner of the New York Giants and it was a most sportsmanlike gesture, typical of Mara. Layden got his salary and the voting for a new commissioner began. Bell at that time was a partner with Art

Rooney in the Pittsburgh Steeler franchise. Rumor had it that
Bell had a contract for Connie Mack Stadium in his pocket, and
if he were denied the commissioner's post he would jump to the
AAFC and start a franchise in Philadelphia to compete against
the Eagles. Whether this was true or not, Bell was elected and
given a three-year contract. After one year the owners tore up
that agreement and gave him a new one for five years; and a
few years later, in 1949, they tore that up and gave him another
for ten years. Never has a commissioner received the respect
and admiration that was accorded Bell.

I became one of Bert Bell's close friends. After peace had
been restored to the pro ranks, Bell asked me to act as chief
adviser and coordinator to the league on matters relating to
radio and television. For twelve seasons, from 1946 to 1958,
I met Bell almost every Monday at the Racquet Club in Philadelphia, where Bell maintained unofficial league offices. We
would have lunch together and Bell would talk to the owners
by telephone. He listened to their problems, sympathized with
them, and when the occasion demanded, would push his view-
points on league matters. Usually, Bert's advice carried.

In 1950, after the leagues had merged, Bell was faced with
the problem of two very weak franchises: the Baltimore Colts
and the New York Yanks, both of the National Conference
(later named the Western Division). The Colts of 1950 won
one game and lost eleven, even with Y. A. Tittle at quarterback.
The Yanks did slightly better but owner Ted Collins was still
losing money. After the 1951 season, Collins finally threw in the
sponge, and Bell, as we have seen, sold the franchise to a syndicate of Texans, with disastrous results.

After the 1950 season, Baltimore president Abe Watner sold
his team to the league and the Colt players were distributed to
other NFL teams. It turned out later that Watner had acted
without authority, and former stockholders of the team threatened suit for the return of the franchise.

My first big job; sportscaster for WJR in Detroit.

This picture was taken at a banquet in Detroit given by "Dick" Richards to honor Eddie Rickenbacker. The linemen are: Ernie McCoy, then Athletic Director at Penn State; the immortal Ty Cobb; Frank Lahey, head coach at Notre Dame; Ken Segler, former Governor of Michigan; John Hanna, president of Michigan State University; and George Halas, coach and owner of the Chicago Bears. The backfield consists of Sid Luckman, quarterback of the Chicago Bears; at left half is famed broadcaster Lowell Thomas; the right half is Alvin "Bo" McMillen, then coach at Indiana and later coach of the Detroit Lions; and the fullback is Eddie Rickenbacker. The coach to the right is "Dick" Richards.

A most unique photograph. That is Henry Ford, Sr. and Harry Bennett relaxing at Willow Run, outside Detroit. Ford, Sr. and Bennett put Willow Run together without a government contract and built the B-24 there. Only after the plane was tested and passed did they get the contract.

My boss at WJR and of the Detroit Lions, G.A. "Dick" Richards at his Palm Springs ranch (1939).

Dick Richards presenting a plaque to J. Edgar Hoover, Director of the FBI, and my good friend. The award was for "Speech-of-the-Year": given by Hoover to the American Legion in 1946.

"Outstanding Young Men of 1946"—Chicago. On my right is the Congressman, John F. Kennedy. Our late President along with myself and eight others won the annual award.

My old roommates, Phil Graham and George Smathers. The picture was taken in 1947.

At the ABC mike in the late '40s when I was director of sports.

This picture tells the story. That's K.S. (Bud) Adams, myself, Lamar Hunt, Robert Housman of Denver, and Sidney Latham, Hunt's attorney. The picture is a UPI wirephoto and was taken on August 14, 1959 in Chicago at Soldiers Field during the All-Star game. Caption read to the effect that a second professional football league was formed that day in Chicago and the people in the picture formed the league.

Mayor Robert Wagner of New York shaking hands with Sammy Baugh. In the background are myself, Bill Shea, and Tom Deegan, top public relations executive from New York. The meeting took place at the 1959 Giants-Colts championship game in Baltimore. Sammy had just become head coach of the New York Titans.

Lamar Hunt and me in Dallas. December 1959. Picture is from the Dallas Morning News, and the caption over the photo read: "The Founders of the American Football League."

Sammy Baugh and I holding the poster of the first Titan home schedule. Picture taken on the patio of my apartment.

The man I respect and admire more than anyone in pro football, George Halas.

Bell had made two mistakes, and he was quick to recognize them. First, he let Collins continue to operate his franchise as a plaything; it became a convenient tax write-off. All clubs suffer when one can't support itself, and with the Yanks' lesson at hand, Bell introduced the concept that a franchise had to represent the major business enterprise of an NFL owner or a competent manager, acceptable to the league, would have to be placed in charge of it. Bell's second error was similar to the first. He allowed a poorly financed and inexperienced group take over the Dallas team. The Dallas fiasco injured the image of pro football in Texas for a number of years.

Bell, in 1953, solved these two problems of franchises in one move. The suit by the Baltimore people was imminent and he had to find places for a group of players from the defunct Dallas Texans. Bell's solution was to transfer the Dallas franchise to Baltimore. Bell, however, was not firmly convinced that Baltimore was a good football town and, under prodding from Marshall, only 25 miles away in Washington, the commissioner insisted that the group demanding the rightful return of the Baltimore franchise sell at least 15,000 season tickets for the upcoming season. A constitutional change giving Marshall various privileges also was necessary before Marshall would agree to the franchise, and a settlement of $150,000 for the Redskins' owner. Bell retained the right to pick the people that eventually would run the franchise.

It was a tough sell for the Baltimore group, especially since they would fall heir to the sorry Dallas team; but by a massive campaign the group sold their tickets and the proceeds of $300,000 were used as operating capital. Bell then picked Carroll Rosenbloom as the chief stockholder and Don Kellett as general manager. Both Rosenbloom and Kellett were close friends of Bell's. All three had graduated from the University of Pennsylvania. As a first payment Rosenbloom paid $13,000 for 51 percent of the stock, and 4 associates put up $3,000 apiece. The remainder of the purchase price, $175,000, was paid out of earnings, already available from the season-ticket sales. Almost immediately he began working out of receipts from season-ticket sales. The deal Rosenbloom got from Bell ranks as one of the best in professional sports.

Actually, Bell almost had to drag Rosenbloom into the league. Carroll was skeptical about the future of Baltimore's franchise, but the success of the season-ticket campaign lent a lot more weight to Bell's pitch. Still, Rosenbloom let it be known from the first that he wasn't going to become involved in running a football club. Even though he had been a player at Penn, he declared that his textile business would keep him too busy to devote much time to the Colts. But, as with all of us, Carroll soon was caught up in the excitement of the game and became one of the most active owners in the league. He is very close to his players.

One of Rosenbloom's partners in other business ventures is Lou Chester from Toronto, who bets huge sums on many sports. It was rumored and even written that Chester and Rosenbloom made a killing, betting on the Colts in the classic 1958 championship game against the Giants. In that game, the Colts had gained possession of the ball in the overtime period after the Giants were stopped short of a first down and had punted. The point spread on the Colts was 3½, and if Chester and Rosenbloom were to win money, the Colts had to beat the Giants by more than 3½ points. With the ball centered on the Giants' 9-yard line, Unitas sent Alan Ameche into the middle for one yard. Then, with everyone expecting the same call, to set up the field goal to win by three, Unitas, one of the great gambling quarterbacks, faked out everyone and threw to Jim Mutscheller in the flat. To prevent an interception, Unitas threw close to the sidelines, and when Mutscheller caught the ball, his momentum carried him out of bounds on the 1. Ameche then cracked over and the Colts had their first NFL championship, won in a game called the "greatest ever played." This game was played and replayed by fan, writer, and broadcaster for months. Speculation was high that Unitas and the Colts went for the touchdown instead of the 3 points because of Rosenbloom's rumored bet. But Unitas silenced the rumors with two sentences: "It's easy to fumble that close to the goal line, with the Giants expecting a run. And anyway, I knew I'd complete the pass!"

Bert Bell was many things but he was never naïve. He never thought that because pro football was a sport, gambling and gamblers couldn't influence the game. He knew people bet on his games and his slant on betting was grown-up. "Let them bet. That's their privilege. My job is to keep it from having an influence on our game."

In 1946, Frank Filchock and Merle Hapes of the New York Giants were approached by gamblers seeking to make sure that the Giants lost to the Bears by more than 10 points in the championship game. Filchock and Hapes turned down the gamblers but failed to report the incident. Increasingly heavy odds for the Bears to win had made the New York City police and Bell suspicious. Earlier in the season, the Giants had beaten the Bears, 14-0, but most experts discounted that loss since the Bears played without George McAfee and some of their other stars. Now all were ready for the Giants. The night before the game, Bell, Police Commissioner Arthur Wallander, and the Maras met with Filchock and Hapes at Mayor Bill O'Dwyer's Gracie Mansion. Filchock and Hapes admitted the offer but denied any complicity. Bell allowed Filchock to play but suspended Hapes. The press got the story the morning of the game. Filchock played a great game for the Giants, even though he was injured, but the Bears won, 24-14—a difference of 10 points.

Bell's action established in the public's mind the idea that gamblers were ever under his watchful eye and could never hope to influence pro football while he was commissioner.

Bell then followed up by hiring an investigating force of former
FBI men to concentrate on gamblers and report to him anything that might involve the league. Bell, unlike some baseball
magnates, didn't bother to have the players trailed. Instead,
he had his staff frequent the haunts of the bookies and gamblers
to find out firsthand if any players, coaches, or owners were
associating with them.

Big money is bet on pro football and most of the bets are
placed on Sunday morning. The bookies don't suspend business
because it's the Sabbath; this is the day to expect the widest
fluctuation in the points. If a star player is hurt or not up to
par, and the news leaks, the Sunday betting would reflect it.
Bell ran his own "wire service," calling all over the league each
Sunday morning and checking his information. If anything
were out of the ordinary, he could know immediately and be in
a position to act. But no matter what safeguards Bert and the
league would put up, there was and is always a way for gamblers to get information. The only way games can be kept free
of outside influence is to count on the integrity of the players
and officials. When you consider the number of years that the
game has been played and the amounts of money that have
been bet, the status of pro football today is testimony not
alone to its popularity but also its honesty.

If I were a gambler and wanted to fix a game, I'd never go to
a player or coach. No one player, not even a quarterback, can
fix a game. Too many situations arise over which the players or
coach have no control. The quarterback would be the most vulnerable because his teammates and coaches would immediately
suspect something if he deviated from the game plans too often
or if his passes were consistently off the mark. The person I
would go to would be an official, probably the umpire. The umpire is the man whose primary duty is to observe the blocking
and the use of hands by both the offense and defense. Players
and coaches say it is almost impossible for a play to be run

without an infraction of some kind. Holding is the usual call and the officials could probably call it every time a play is run. If my partner in crime were the umpire, he could control the scoring by dropping his flag whenever the wrong team scored.

There is another logical reason why the officials would be the ones to try to fix. They are underpaid and overcriticized. They are a perfect target for a player or a coach who is anxious to alibi on a poor performance. And if pro football doesn't protect these men from attacks and make their jobs more financially attractive, it will lose many of the good ones and the level of the game will deteriorate.

Bell was aware that such a situation might develop as early as 1951, when many coaches and owners were blaming the officials for their own mistakes and misfortunes. Typically, his response was direct and unequivocal: "Stop talking about the officials or I'll quit." The criticism stopped.

After World War II, television—the "magic box" or the "boob-tube" if you will—began to come into its own and to change the living habits of all Americans. And if television's impact was felt in the field of news and entertainment, its influence on sports was and is tremendous. For boxing, it meant quick riches and a slow death. For baseball it meant the end of most of the minor leagues and the beginning of public apathy toward the game. For football, TV has been a bonanza.

There are and will be many memorials to Bert Bell, and all are deserved, but the owners, players, officials, and fans should all thank their lucky stars that Bert Bell was on the scene when television came along. Without Bell, I think pro football would have suffered the same fate as boxing.

I worked closely with Bell and the other owners in developing radio and television outlets for pro football. In the late Forties and early Fifties, television agreements were entered into by several clubs. We studied the results closely, and it became apparent that the gate was affected whenever the home game was televised locally or if a game was televised into an area where another game was being played.

In 1952, the NFL by-laws were amended to provide that no telecast or broadcast could be made within 75 miles of another league city on the day when that home team was playing, either at home or away. The government contended that the NFL was exercising an illegal restraint on the interstate business of radio and television, under the antitrust code. The by-laws also gave the NFL commissioner unlimited power to make contracts in the name of all clubs acting in concert, and to ban or permit television or broadcasting at his whim. This, too, the Justice Department maintained, was a violation.

The Justice Department began to pressure the league to do away with these practices, and many of the owners wanted to give in. Bell was adamant. He told me that if we gave up the blackout, we would be giving up pro football. He pleaded with the owners not to back down, and finally they agreed to take their case to court. The United States then brought action against the NFL to enjoin it from following its blackout practices, and the case was heard by Judge Alan Grim in the U.S. District Court for eastern Pennsylvania.

Judge Grim rendered his decision on November 12, 1953. In an opinion notable for its grasp of sports procedure, both on the field and in the front office, the justice ruled that the blackout was not an unreasonable restraint of interstate commerce. Judge Grim pointed out that "the purposes of the Sherman Act certainly will not be served by prohibiting the defendant clubs, particularly the weaker clubs, from protecting their home gate receipts from the disastrous financial effects of invading telecasts of outside games." However, Grim ruled out any interference with radio and enjoined Bell from interfering with, or controlling, the making of contracts by the separate clubs. The commissioner also was restrained from controlling the television contracts of the clubs, but this injunction was lifted in 1962 by a federal law which permitted NFL clubs to act in concert under direction of their commissioner.

I never knew Bell to be so elated as he was by the Grim decision. He had a right to be, because the blackout had been saved, and the NFL had obtained a *modus operandi* for unlimited success in the future. If Bert had not done anything else for the league, this court decision would have made his name memorable.

Bert Bell died in 1959, watching his beloved Eagles play at Franklin Field. I lost a close friend and pro football lost its greatest leader.

PART IV

THE AMERICAN FOOTBALL LEAGUE

I had been broadcasting the Redskins' games for years and had been a close friend of George and Corinne Marshall, but it wasn't until I became a part owner of the 'Skins that I began disagreeing with George over the operation of the club. I had watched the team go downhill steadily since 1945, and even the element of competition with the AAFC didn't answer the many questions fans were raising over the 'Skins poor showing.

As the 'Skins broadcaster I still talked as if they were the greatest, as if only the "breaks" kept them from winning. But as a stockholder, I knew a lot was wrong and exercised my rights by criticizing Marshall to his face. I was familiar with the 'Skins' operations and personnel as was Marshall. My differences with him revolved around poor coaching, his failure to draft Negroes, and his treatment of Vic Janowicz. Corinne backed me on all these matters, especially the coaching situation. Both of us reasoned that if the 'Skins had been winners under Ray Flaherty, why not hire him again now that he was free. Marshall would roar his dislike of Flaherty and we would roar back, and these scenes undoubtedly widened the break between Marshall and me, and between Marshall and Corinne.

But if coaching was an issue, it was small compared to the

59

question of the draft. Marshall refused to draft or sign a Negro
player. He maintained that his fans and viewing audience were
southern and white and insisted that they would boycott the
stadium and the team if he were to start signing Negroes. He
was wrong, he knew he was wrong, refused to admit it, and
blamed all the Redskins' failures on everyone but himself.
Negro stars were in key spots on all other NFL teams. Jimmy
Brown at Cleveland, Lenny Moore at Baltimore, Ollie Matson
at Chicago and Los Angeles, John Henry Johnson at Pittsburgh, and many others were national sports celebrities, not
merely eastern or western or midwestern heroes. Had Marshall
drafted or dealt for top Negro players, the 'Skins would have
regained their old championship ways, because there were still
some fine players on the team in the Fifties.

To be critical of Marshall in the press or over radio was to
create an enemy. Shirley Povich of the *Washington Post* found
that out when he once criticized Marshall in a column for
making the players sit up all night on the train home from a
game to save money, even though Pullman berths were available. After that, Povich and Marshall were bitter enemies.

In 1956, after our annual exhibition with the Rams in Los
Angeles, Vic Janowicz took his date to a team party. Janowicz
was a Heisman Trophy winner while at Ohio State and a star of
the 'Skins. On the way to the party, they were involved in an
auto accident. The girl was unharmed but Janowicz was seriously injured and his football career was finished. The year before, Janowicz had excelled for us and had been the team's
leading scorer; but when he was hurt, Marshall cut him off the
payroll because the accident hadn't occurred in the line of
duty. Although Janowicz was not on the payroll when the
season opened, he did sit on Joe Kuharich's bench in our game
against the Cardinals in Chicago. It was, of course, a way for
the team to show their scorn for Marshall. I understood that
the players were contributing to make up Vic's salary and I

asked Kuharich to put me down for $200 a week, with a
promise to make up anything lacking at the end of the season.
I felt that Marshall's handling of the whole situation had been
needlessly cruel. I said so on my network radio show, even
though I realize now that I was violating the broadcasters' code
and that Marshall would be livid about it.

After the incident we were barely on speaking terms. Our
falling out was complete when I later asked for a financial
accounting on the ballclub. George refused. There had been no
dividends distributed on the stock since I bought it, and he had
turned aside all my efforts to get a satisfactory explanation. By
this time it was apparent I would have to bow out as the 'Skins'
announcer, since I could no longer stomach the tactics of Marshall and still be enthusiastic about the team on the radio. In
1957 I sued Marshall for $500,000, and the case dragged on
until 1960, when I sold my 25 percent holdings in the 'Skins.
The transaction was held in the office of Clark Clifford. Present
were Tom MacShaine, partner of Clifford, Milton King, a 5 percent owner of the 'Skins and Mr. Nordlinger. King and Nordlinger had a cashier's check for $350,000, which they gave me.
I turned over my stock to them and we called off the suit.
Months later I learned that the money came from Jack Cooke
of Toronto and he became the largest minority stockholder in
the Redskins.

My farewell to Marshall and the Redskins, if not happy, was
at least loud. Marshall's friend Tom Gallery, then sports director of NBC, was present when we said good-bye. I left with
Marshall's warning in my ears: "We'll get you. We'll break
you!" I assumed the "we" meant he and Gallery. I didn't understand Gallery's feelings, since I had been a friend of his in the
days before NBC.

Marshall and Gallery meant what they said. In 1957 I broadcast for television the following sporting events: the NFL
championship game, the Sugar Bowl game, the East-West

game, the NFL Pro Bowl game, the North-South game, the
Masters Golf Tournament, and the National Open. In addition
I was doing Notre Dame football, the Redskins' games and, for
the Mutual Broadcasting System, a network radio show five
nights a week. I also did a fifteen-minute show after every
Brooklyn Dodger home game.

In 1958 I lost all of those events except my Mutual sports
show and the Dodger games. Most of the major sporting events
were then televised by NBC. Gallery was director of sports for
the network and he must have worked long and hard to have me
dropped. In radio and television, the network has a team of announcers and it usually assigns one of the staff to a game. They
then charge the sponsor a fee for that announcer's services,
keeping the fee themselves because they pay the announcers a
straight salary. Chris Schenkel, one of the best in the business,
works for ABC. They pay him a salary. They then assign Schenkel as many sporting events as he can handle and charge the
sponsor a fee each time for Chris' services to make up for the
salary they are paying him. But if the sponsor insists on a particular announcer, the network will fight for their man, not the
sponsor's, and usually the network will prevail unless the sponsor is powerful enough to bend the network to his will. For
years I had worked closely with L. B. Iseley of Wilson Sporting
Goods, Fred Miller of the Miller Brewing Company, Eugene
Grace of Bethlehem Steel, and Charles O'Neil of General Tire.
These men were the presidents of the companies sponsoring
most of the major sporting events that were broadcast. All were
good friends of mine. But during the Fifties most of them
passed on. Fred Miller died in a plane accident. He and his only
son were going on a hunting trip in northern Wisconsin when
his private plane went down. We had talked before a game at
Notre Dame a week earlier and had made plans for dinner in
New York the next week. When I heard his private plane had
gone down near Milwaukee, I literally cried. Fred Miller was

one of the finest men I ever knew. A great player at Notre Dame, he was instrumental in keeping the Packers going in the Forties and was the leader of the move to bring the baseball Braves to Milwaukee.

It's ironic that these good friends all died within a few years, and just at the time Gallery and Marshall were scheming to get me. And how they succeeded! By 1959 all I had left were the Notre Dame games and my Mutual show. They didn't break me, but they sure roughed me up.

In the winter of 1957, the word had leaked that Walter O'Malley was going to move his Brooklyn Dodger baseball franchise to Los Angeles and that Horace Stoneham would take the Giants to San Francisco. I started a drive over the local Mutual station in New York to "keep the Dodgers in Brooklyn." The campaign caught on and soon O'Malley was swamped with letters protesting his move and begging him to keep the Dodgers in Brooklyn. The newspaper columnists jumped on O'Malley, but nothing we did or said could stop him. Los Angeles wanted them so badly they gave O'Malley everything but slave labor to help in the transfer. I can understand O'Malley's move. He's a lawyer and banker, not a sportsman. The move, to him, was logical and smart from a business standpoint. He has made a fortune from it.

O'Malley began his career with the Dodgers as the watchdog lawyer assigned by the Brooklyn Trust Company to watch the Dodger account. The man who assigned O'Malley was George V. McLaughlin, president of Brooklyn Trust and former police commissioner of New York City. O'Malley did his job so well that he ended up gaining control of the Dodgers in 1948.

Before the Dodgers had been kissed by their first movie star, plans were under way to replace the Dodgers and Giants in New York. McLaughlin was talking up a team to replace the Dodgers almost before they left, and pretty soon William A.

"Bill" Shea was empowered by Mayor Robert Wagner to do something about it. Shea headed the Mayor's Baseball Committee, with James A. Farley, Bernard J. Gimbel, and Clinton Blume his colleagues.

Shea was an associate of O'Malley under McLaughlin in the Thirties but left the bank about 1940 to help found the firm of Manning, Hollinger, and Shea, of which eventually he became senior partner. He became a major sports figure in 1958 when asked to fill the void that his ex-associate's pull-out had left.

Born in 1907 in New York, Shea attended grammar school in Brooklyn and high school in upper Manhattan, then enrolled at New York University. After one year he switched to Georgetown on a football scholarship that extended over the full five years he needed to complete his law studies.

In May of 1958 the Shea committee predicted that the Flushing Stadium could be constructed for as little as $12 million in conjunction with other authorized improvements, mainly roads, for the projected World's Fair on the adjoining meadows. I wondered at the time how such a comparatively small sum of money could be made to stretch into a modern stadium of 60,000 capacity. My wonder was justified. The figure was revised to $18 million soon thereafter, and estimates went as high as $25 million while the stadium was being built. Insiders say the final cost was $42,000,000! There has been some talk recently of equipping Shea Stadium with a dome. It seems unlikely. Those books had best remain closed.

While the new stadium was still in the idea stage, I often met with McLaughlin, and at one of our get-togethers he told me that there was a possibility that a new football league would soon be formed and that if anything more definite developed he would be in touch with me.

In the spring of 1959, the stadium drive was dragging. Shea had received no encouragement from the National League that it would return to New York, and with Branch Rickey he had begun assembling the Continental League in November of 1958.

The way I heard it from baseball men, the Continental faced almost insurmountable obstacles, and many surmised that it was simply a gimmick of Shea's to put pressure on the National League to return to New York. Whatever the Continental would have been, the majors at least recognized its nuisance value by knocking it out in August 1960, absorbing four of its franchises, and expanding to two 10-club leagues.

I had known Bill Shea for some time. His father-in-law is Tom Shaw, who was reputed to be the biggest legalized bookmaker in New York. Bill had once run a minor league football franchise, the Long Island Indians, which had folded. He was the attorney for the NFL team (mentioned earlier) owned by Ted Collins that was known variously as the Boston Yanks, New York Bulldogs, and New York Yanks. Collins dropped about $800,000 before calling it quits.

Shea and I finally got together to discuss football at the Sands Point Country Club on Long Island. He noted that McLaughlin and I were good friends, and that he and McLaughlin were good friends, and said he hoped we could work together with me heading a new football club in New York City. Shea named Lamar Hunt of Dallas as his contact and inquired whether he could have Hunt look me up.

The answer had to be "yes." I had spent practically my whole working life in the pros. I had holdings in the Detroit Lions and the Washington Redskins at that time, and naturally I was interested in anything connected with the sport. Shea emphasized that a football as well as a baseball tenant was necessary to attract investors and financial support from the city, a war cry I soon began to know by heart. He brought up financing by saying that he knew I'd made a million in the market in Brunswick stock and advised me to start lining up some important people. "If you can't," he continued, "the mayor, McLaughlin, and I, and other people in the community will come up with something. We know that it will take a lot to make it go." I did not press Shea about money, and he never made a firm commitment at any time to bring in any specific sum. I assumed that he would help as he had indicated.

I met Lamar Hunt in July of 1959 at the Belmont Plaza Hotel in New York. With him was Davey O'Brien, the former great passer of Bert Bell's Philadelphia Eagles. I didn't know Lamar but I had met his father, Haroldson Lafayette Hunt, reputed to be the richest man in the country. I first met the senior Hunt at a party given by Ray Ryan, an old friend of mine. Ryan is one of the biggest gamblers in the country and called the senior Hunt "his pigeon." There was nothing phony about Hunt. He had made his fortune by borrowing $50 and betting he could find oil on land where the geologists said there wasn't any. H. L. Hunt's philosophy of life was that a man would succeed if he kept plugging and was willing to gamble. Ryan told me he thought that H.L. bet close to a million dollars a week during the football season. That's a staggering sum to most but a drop in the bucket to him. Ryan would entertain me for hours with stories about H. L. Hunt. Ray Ryan himself is a pretty salty character and owns the Mt. Kenya Sportsman's Club in Africa. His partner is Bill Holden, the movie star. Lamar Hunt was the opposite of his father in personality. Lamar often wore shoes with holes in the soles and seemed to take particular pains to cross his legs when he sat down so that the holes would be noticeable to everyone in the room. Perhaps he felt that this display of poverty would somehow lift from his shoulders the stigma of his and his father's enormous wealth. But if his money made him uneasy, he certainly showed no inclination to part with any of it.

My first meeting with Lamar lasted about two hours. He did most of the talking, telling me he wanted to start another football league and that he had heard that I was the best man to have as a partner in organizing and publicizing the new league. I told Lamar I was already part owner of two teams in the NFL, though he didn't believe me. He thought it was against the NFL rules for a person to have interests in more than one team. I told him that he was mistaken and informed him that the Cardinals had been part owners of the Bears for years.

I asked him who else he had contacted and what cities he thought would join. He stated he had just talked with Bud Adams of Houston and he wanted to be included. Adams' father owned Phillips Oil and Bud, the Ada Oil Company. Hunt said he also had approached Max Winter of Minneapolis and Winter was putting together a group to start a franchise. Winter owned the Minneapolis Lakers basketball team. Another prospect was Denver, where Hunt had lined up Bob Howsam, who was remodeling the Denver Bears' stadium, which he owned, on the assumption that the Continental Baseball League would play there. Last was Los Angeles, where Hunt was sure that Barron Hilton, stepson of Conrad Hilton, would come in. Hunt in Dallas made five and if I came in with New York, that would give us six.

Hunt wanted to know, finally, whether I would come in with him, and stressed my ability to "generate publicity and controversy." I told him I would be willing to look into it, but added that I felt the financial responsibility ought to be spelled out. My talks with McLaughlin, Shea, Newbold Morris, and Mayor Wagner led me to believe that I would be the ideal person to start a new team, but that I was not to pick up the entire bill. The way I interpreted it, I would "front" for the franchise and participate to a certain extent financially, and they would supply fresh capital when needed.

Ever since McLaughlin had first mentioned a second New York team and another league to me, I had tried to picture its chances of success compared with the fate of the All America Football Conference. I went over the matter with Hunt, although he was only twenty-six at the time, and knew of the AAFC solely by hearsay. The AAFC had had an open shot at star talent coming up to its inaugural in 1946, whereas the league Hunt had proposed would have to buck a market in which the established players were virtually monopolized by the NFL. Our prospect, as we saw it in 1959, was quite different. The NFL had a tight grip on its athletes, although they could elect to be "freed" on a year's notice. That is, a player signed a contract for one year, with an option for a second season. After the first year, however, he did not have to sign again. He could merely work out the option season in the original contract and could sign with any other club anywhere, without fear of court action. Hunt and I agreed we could not count on "option" players; that method was too speculative. We would have to bid against the NFL for college stars, meanwhile picking up whatever strays there might be. Perhaps we might resort to raiding, if necessary, but Hunt and I from the start were firmly against any sort of contract-busting that could land us in court. Raiding shaped up as impractical, costly, and troublesome.

But if talent procurement was a minus, there were two potential plusses for a rival league. First was the likelihood of television revenue, and second, there was the popularity of pro football. The AAFC had enjoyed neither of these advantages. I felt that the competition for advertising space on NFL telecasts might turn some of the disappointed sponsors who were unable to buy space to our side. Hunt was delighted with the prospect.

During the first five years of the AFL's existence television revenue kept the league alive and then gave it a life-insurance policy; that is, provided sponsors buy the NBC package for 1965-70. Gate receipts, though, were very spotty; and although the Eastern Division seems headed for success in its sixth year, the entire Western Division of San Diego, Denver, Kansas City, and Oakland has been one vast money-losing morass.

There was no way for us to anticipate this picture in 1959; we had no idea then that we would wind up with franchises in

Oakland, San Diego, and Kansas City. Enthusiasm no doubt colored our estimates, but Hunt and I did think that a new league properly organized and financed would have a chance, even against the powerfully entrenched NFL. Lamar asked me to arrange a meeting with Bert Bell for Davey and him. I phoned Bell—he was at his summer retreat in Atlantic City— and he agreed to see Hunt and O'Brien. Bert met anybody and everybody; I never knew him to turn down a soul, by phone or in person. For another thing, I fancy Bert thought he could learn what Hunt was planning. After I had hung up, I advised O'Brien and Hunt to hire a car and get to Atlantic City as fast as possible. Hunt objected—a bus would be cheaper. I should have seen the handwriting on the wall. I hired a Carey limousine for them over Hunt's protests, and they were off to their appointment with Bell. I paid the rental on the car.

On the return trip Hunt and O'Brien had the driver drop them off at Newark Airport and Lamar phoned me from there. He said they had a very friendly and profitable chat with Bell, and that the commissioner said he had no objections whatever to another league. In fact, Hunt added, Bell thought it might be a good thing. Hunt did not seem to comprehend that Bell could not afford to denounce the forthcoming league, even if he were so disposed. He was not likely to risk the suspicion that the NFL would act to preserve a practical monopoly. Perhaps the shrewd old man sized up his man and gave Hunt no ammunition whatever for the lawsuit he filed later. Bell actually offered sound advice to Hunt and to others in the AFL on the operation of a franchise. At no time was he uncommunicative or devious, and at all times he maintained his usual genial front.

After Lamar called from Newark, I gave the matter serious thought and a few days later called Shea and McLaughlin to tell them of Hunt's visit and proposal. I had decided to help Hunt start his league by forming a franchise in New York for

the AFL. When Shea and McLaughlin heard the news, they
were delighted and said that the new stadium was now a
certainty and to call them for any assistance possible. I then
called Hunt and told him I was coming in. He was as pleased
as Shea and McLaughlin had been and immediately asked me
to take over and set up a meeting. I suggested a meeting in
Chicago during All-Star week, when writers and coaches from
all over the country would be in town for the pre-game fes-
tivities.

On August 14, 1959, the American Football League was
founded in the Conrad Hilton Hotel in Chicago. The AP and
UPI honored my request for coverage, and pictures of our
group were wired coast-to-coast. Many writers from many
cities inquired about our organization, and the meeting gave
us our first solid public exposure.

There were no earthshaking decisions made at the meeting,
because it was merely formative, to line up our members for the
first time, acquaint them with one another's thinking, and let
them project the future as clearly as possible. Nevertheless, I
felt so strongly about rivalries that I made a strong appeal for
careful consideration of our seventh and eighth franchises. My
belief was that New York and Minneapolis, two strongholds of
football and population, could not be left without natural rivals.

In New York I had to undertake the formidable task of com-
peting against the Giants of the NFL, and I wanted to have at
least one good attraction to present. Being from Michigan, and
steeped in Big Ten football, I admit I may have been partial to
the Midwest, but I really couldn't see our league succeeding
without strong representation in the nation's football heartland.

The most necessary element in pro sports is the natural
rivalry, the spontaneous interest that arises when two cities of
comparative size in the same area of the country sponsor teams
in the same league. We had, to be sure, the great rivalry between Dallas and Houston, but then came an odd assortment of

Los Angeles, Denver, Minneapolis, and New York. Can you imagine brewing up a nice spicy feud between Denver and New York? Or Minneapolis and Los Angeles? This matter of sectional rivalries was urgent to me, but we had to put it off until a later date when the field of possible franchises could be reviewed. The members were willing to proceed with a six-club league in 1960, if necessary, but that issue was almost academic because it seemed likely that we would bow in with eight.

At our second meeting in Dallas, on August 22, I made a strong case for the inclusion of an eastern club or two in the league, citing Buffalo and Boston, to set up one of those sectional rivalries which had proved to be the strength of the NFL. For examples I mentioned the poison-ivy classics between the Chicago Bears and the Green Bay Packers in the Midwest, and between the Washington Redskins and the New York Giants in the East. The NFL was able to survive on the national appeal of these two highly popular series until other clubs were firmly established.

At our third meeting in Beverly Hills, September 12, the prospect of gaining Boston grew bright, because William H. Sullivan assured us that he soon would have a package to present. I sold Sullivan on joining the league and he sold the rest of his people.

Then, at our fourth meeting, in my New York apartment, on October 28, we brought in Ralph C. Wilson, Jr., of Buffalo as our seventh franchise holder. We were riding high, it seemed, because the AFL was nearing a full complement of eight clubs; and I had a special reason for celebrating because my colleagues had given my team, the Titans, a natural geographic rival when they approved Buffalo.

Buffalo may have been lucky to get the franchise, because Wilson at first wanted to play in Miami, but he could not get permission to use the Orange Bowl. I called Senator Smathers and others to ask their help and, though they tried valiantly, it was to no avail.

Because of my interest in another northern or eastern franchise, I looked up Pete Crotty, Democratic leader of Erie County in New York, who recently spearheaded Bob Kennedy's drive to the U.S. Senate. He was very obliging when I went to Buffalo to appraise the situation and offered the stadium at a very reasonable rate.

Buffalo had been a staunch member of the All America Conference and had tried vainly to enter the NFL ever since 1949. The city had always ranked high in football interest, but its weather was always held against it. However, weather is a problem in November in the whole tier of northern clubs in the NFL. Anyway, from 'way back, football has always been considered a game to be played in any weather.

I had known Ralph Wilson, Sr. since my Detroit days, through Dick Richards. I saw him often at the Detroit A.C., the Bloomfield Hills Country Club, and the Detroit Country Club, near their home in Grosse Point. Young Ralph attended the University of Virginia and the University of Michigan Law School before enlisting in the Navy in World War II. Then he followed his father into insurance and trucking. Though I knew the senior Wilson, I was not acquainted with young Ralph. When I first heard he was to join us, I called John Tompkins, director of American Airlines, in Detroit and one of the directors of the Buffalo franchise. Tompkins has been a civic leader in Detroit for years and has been on the committee that has tried valiantly to bring the 1968 Olympics to the Motor City. John told me about Ralph Wilson, Jr., and said he was first rate in every way and, most important, he had the financial wherewithal to handle a football franchise. Wilson had always had a keen interest in pro football, and he had been a small stockholder in the Detroit

Lions while I was one of seven largest. Ralph and I never met until we began the AFL.

The Wilson family fortune probably runs to $100 million, but Ralph Wilson, Sr., did it the hard way, by going broke and bouncing back three times. Ralph, Sr., doesn't look or act old, and enjoys telling people how he hit the deck so often and got up every time.

Sullivan formed a syndicate with nine other Boston business-men. They were Dom DiMaggio, former Red Sox baseball star, Dan Marr, Joseph E. Sullivan, Paul Sonnabend, Edgar L. Turner, Dean Boylan, Ed McMann, John Ames, Jr., and George Sargent.

Sullivan's main coup, however, was to float a public-stock issue for the Patriots in Boston. The syndicate thereby took in $500,000 from the public, after broker's fees, without yielding an iota of control in the operation. The issue was entirely non-voting. Furthermore, it was doubtful in those formative days whether anybody would pay $500,000 for a franchise. I have been asked many times why I never offered Titan stock for public sale and the question always makes me smile. New Yorkers are great gamblers, but they have the big board, the American Exchange, and the mutuels, and it would have been practically impossible to sell them an untried football stock.

When the meeting closed I invited Wilson and his wife Janet to El Morocco for dinner, along with Lamar Hunt, who was staying at my place. We were enjoying ourselves, chatting and drinking, when Hunt asked to be excused, saying he had to catch a plane to California. Wilson and I were both surprised, because we had planned to go over some league matters with Lamar the next morning. I took him to my place, and while he packed I checked on a composite list of airline flights and saw that no planes were leaving for the Coast until morning. I became suspicious and called John J. Broady, a detective friend

of mine, and asked him to go to Idlewild to find out where
Hunt was going. Underhanded? Perhaps. But I had invested
a lot of money in the future of the AFL and I wanted to be
sure of my co-founder. Hunt took a cab to Idlewild and I
returned to El Morocco. Broady called an hour later saying
Hunt had boarded a plane for Chicago. To me that meant only
one thing. Hunt was going to see George Halas.

Broady had given me the flight number and time of arrival,
which was about 10:30 P.M. Central Standard time, and in five
or ten minutes I had alerted the news services in Chicago that
a distinguished visitor was heading their way. I tipped them
off that Halas was probably involved, and the editors assured
me they would track down the quarry. They got a bonus—Bud
Adams of Houston also arrived for the caucus with Halas and
Hunt. They met at the Illinois Athletic Club.

Both Hunt and Adams had long been eager for NFL franchises. That was only natural. But if they were playing games
and running the league as a bluff with a patsy like me as a
spear-carrier, then I had to find out. The Continental Baseball
League turned out on that order a year later.

All applications for new NFL franchises had to be cleared
through Halas, chairman of the expansion committee. When I
discovered that Hunt was going to Chicago on the sly to meet
Halas, and that Adams had joined them here, all doubts about
their motives vanished from my mind.

In 1958, both Hunt and Adams, along with Bob Howsam of
Denver and H. P. Skoglund of Minneapolis, had been advised
by Bert Bell that no NFL expansion was anticipated before
1961. Then, in February of 1959, Halas and Art Rooney of
Pittsburgh, the other member of the expansion committee, announced that both Dallas and Houston were likely sites for
new NFL franchises, Rooney adding, after a visit to Houston,
that that city would be preferable. Buffalo, Miami, and Minne-

apolis also were mentioned. According to Halas, although he had no explicit authority for such a statement from his fellow owners, 1961–65 would be the era of expansion. In April, Halas followed up by informing Craig Cullinan, who had been associated with Adams in his unsuccessful bid for a Houston NFL franchise in 1957, that he was back in the running. Around the same time, Hunt quizzed Halas again about a Dallas franchise.

In June of 1959 Hunt privately decided to form a new league with Adams. A few days later, Hunt and O'Brien had their conference with Bell and Hunt then began collecting his league. Soon thereafter, the NFL commissioner announced on July 28 to a congressional committee that was studying one of the endless succession of sports bills that never pass, that the formation of a new league was imminent. Bob Howsam, already an AFL member, stole into Philadelphia for a confab with Bell on August 18. I never did learn what he was up to. It didn't matter much in the end, because Howsam unfortunately was socked twice—by Bill Shea's Continental League and by the AFL.

Things were happening fast. On August 29, Halas and Rooney advised Clint Murchison who, along with Clint, Jr., had been trying to buy my Redskins stock since 1952, and his associate, Bedford Wynne, that Dallas would be eligible for NFL membership in 1960, to start even up with Hunt's AFL team. They told the Cullinan group that Houston would be admitted at the same time provided Rice University stadium was available.

Meanwhile, in the Pacific theater of action, Barron Hilton may have begun to have some doubts about bucking the established Rams in the Los Angeles Coliseum. Ed Pauley, wealthy partner in the Rams and a friend of Hilton, advised Barron that he would be better off to buy a share in his club because two clubs in one arena simply would not succeed. Hilton went along with the AFL, however, and played the first year in direct competition with the Rams in the Coliseum before moving his franchise to San Diego.

Throughout the summer and into the fall the maneuvering continued. Hunt of our AFL met his Dallas opponents in the NFL, Murchison and Wynne, in early September. Hilton brought in Adams for another chat with Pauley about the same time. Max Winter, Twin Cities promoter who was in the Minneapolis syndicate holding an AFL franchise, looked up both Halas and Rooney.

On the AFL antitrust suit against the NFL, Federal Judge Roszel Thomsen commented that "All of the AFL men, with the possible exception of Hunt, would still have preferred NFL franchises; many of them would have been satisfied with a substantial interest in an NFL franchise."

I differ with the judge in particulars. I feel sure that Hunt wanted an NFL franchise down to the last, when he turned against the older league with his court suit. Also, I did not fit into the Judge's picture because I had substantial interests in two NFL franchises.

On October 11, Bell died and Halas took over. In a meeting following the Bell funeral, George got the votes of all clubs but Washington for an unspecified expansion. On October 19, Halas stated that the NFL would admit two teams in 1960 and two more in 1961 or 1962. Obviously this was a propaganda stratagem; the NFL never seriously considered such a rapid expansion. Later that month, Murchison offered a partnership in the Dallas franchise to Hunt and wondered whether the AFL would disband if Adams, the Minneapolis group, Wilson, and Hunt were accommodated in some way by the NFL. Lamar told Murchison that he was committed to his partners in the AFL, that he could not jettison New York, Los Angeles, and Denver without risking a lawsuit. In November, 1959, Hunt and Murchison had a conference with Carroll Rosenbloom in

New York; Hunt saw Halas in Los Angeles; and Hunt and Adams, as mentioned, caught George in Chicago.

At the tremendously important meeting at Minneapolis, set for November 22, 1959, we were going to admit Boston as our eighth city and go through our draft of college players. After the Minneapolis meeting, our owners would start moving around the country signing players and filling out front office and coaching staffs, and we would be ready to undergo the usual grind of trial-and-error in training camp that produces a team.

Most of our owners intended to arrive in Minneapolis late Saturday, November 21, and attend an NFL game in Met Stadium between the Chicago Cardinals and the New York Giants on Sunday afternoon. Then we would open our meeting about 8 P.M.

The Cardinals were doing poorly in Comiskey Park in Chicago and had farmed out two of their home games to Minneapolis, counting on football fever there to bolster their sagging gate. The fact that the Cardinals could go into neutral Minneapolis and draw well made me think more highly than ever of our Minneapolis franchise. I only wished we had another Midwestern club to provide a rival for Minneapolis.

The three men who held the Minneapolis franchise had been present at all AFL league meetings from the start and took a working interest in our affairs. H.P. Skoglund was on the committee to select a commissioner, Max Winter was in charge of the upcoming draft, and E. William Boyer was on the committee to draft a constitution.

They were three diverse types. Skoglund was heavy-set, about 240 pounds, with the usual unsophisticated appearance of a man of affairs in the old-country area of the old Northwest. He had made his way from clerk to president of an insurance company in four years as a young man, and now, in his sixties, he had wide interests.

Winter was a lean, wary-looking chap who had come from Austria and attended the University of Chicago before going into the automobile business in Minnesota. From that start he branched into the sports business as a promoter, to bring various national attractions into the Twin Cities area. He owned the Minneapolis Lakers basketball team and I had heard he was friendly with most of the gambling interests in Minnesota.

Boyer, a tall, forceful, outspoken man was chairman of the Minneapolis Chamber of Commerce and also a partner in an auto distributorship. Boyer was shrewd and wily, the very characteristics his jobs demanded.

I was unable to reach Minneapolis on Saturday, as I was broadcasting the game between Notre Dame and Iowa at Iowa City, so I flew to Chicago, then made a morning connection for the Twin Cities. I got up early and phoned Frank Leahy, the former Notre Dame coach, at Minneapolis. Frank was general manager of the Los Angeles Chargers and had assured me he would arrive early Saturday to help Winter set up draft assignments. Leahy told me that something was wrong. He couldn't put his finger on it but said that there was too much NFL news appearing in the papers. Leahy knew all the sportswriters well, and some of them had hinted to him to be alert for sleeper moves. If Leahy was worried, so was I, for Frank was too experienced a man in big-time sports to worry easily or needlessly. I called Mims Thomason, president of UPI, at his home in Connecticut and told him of Frank's concern. I asked him to check his sources and to call me in Minneapolis if he could uncover any information. Mims said he would be glad to oblige.

By the time I reached Minneapolis, Leahy had become even more agitated. He was sure that Winter and Boyer were giving us the run-around. We were unable to do anything that afternoon, because all of our associates were at the Giants-Cardinals game.

Our Minneapolis hosts had arranged dinner for us at Cedric Adams' restaurant, but there was no privacy provided. The AFL owners were set on a dais in a large room with about 200 members of booster clubs, who apparently had been invited to look us over. I sat with Hunt on one side and Winter on the other, and dinner had just begun when I was called to the phone.

Mims Thomason was on the line. His words hit me like lightning. "Harry, you're being taken. We have received a tip that the NFL has offered a franchise to Minneapolis and it has been accepted. Your people are out!"

I didn't, couldn't, say anything. I was stunned. Mims went on to tell me that the *New York Sunday Mirror* was carrying a story by Harold Weisman stating that the AFL had "died in childbirth" in Minneapolis. If Weisman had the story, had written a column about it, he would have had to have known of it on Saturday, because his paper's Sunday deadline was 8 P.M. Saturday night.

Mims was right. We'd been had. Halas had finally made his move. I was sick. I went back into the dining room, my sickness rapidly giving way to rage. I walked to the center of the dais and asked for quiet. "Ladies and gentlemen, I think that so far as the AFL is concerned in Minneapolis, this is our Last Supper."

The room exploded, and so did Hunt. He demanded an explanation, so I took him outside the room, along with Winter. I grabbed Winter by the lapels of his coat and roared at him to open up about the NFL deal. Winter denied everything; Hunt was yelling at me to take it easy; I was telling Hunt to shut up and trying to wring the truth out of Winter. Finally Winter began to nod his head to my questions. He was almost hysterical now, and stammered that he, Boyer, and Skoglund had asked for an NFL franchise and he thought they had one.

I turned to Hunt and told him what Mims had said and mentioned the Weisman column. Hunt didn't grasp the significance of all this, but I was too emotionally spent to explain. Winter left, dinner broke up, and we all returned to the hotel for the formal meeting. I rode back to the hotel with Boyer and asked him point-blank if he and his cronies were doublecrossing us. He mumbled something about not feeling well, and since his son was driving the car, I didn't push the matter. Boyer dropped me off at the hotel and went home.

In the suite, our owners were there, along with Skoglund and Winter. Hunt called the meeting to order and began with some idiotic nonsense about rules of order, at which point I jumped up and demanded that Winter and Skoglund tell the meeting whether they were joining the AFL or the NFL. They looked at Hunt to see if they should answer. Hunt didn't know what to do, so he advised me to take it easy. If we took it any easier, we were finished. Hunt obviously was at a loss to act, so I did. I demanded that Winter show me the telegram he had received from Halas. Winter just looked at Hunt. The tip-off on the telegram had come from Leahy. I repeated my demand, and when Winter still remained silent I told him to get out. He left, and suddenly the meeting broke up. All was bedlam. I just sat there, but I'll never forget the stunned look on Billy Sullivan's face. He had come to Minneapolis to join the AFL, and his hosts were jumping to the other league.

Someone brought in the early edition of the *Minneapolis Tribune* and the headlines carried the grim story: the NFL had assured the Twin Cities a franchise in 1960. Charlie Johnson, the sports editor, had written the story, and since he had led the move to bring major league baseball and an NFL franchise to Minneapolis, his words had to be true.

With the story in front of us, it was now or never for the AFL. If we adjourned without deciding whether or not to continue with our draft, I'm sure the league would not have lasted another day. Hunt still hadn't said or done anything, and Sullivan was still too stunned to talk. But Ralph Wilson, Bud Adams, Barron Hilton, and I were willing to fight. Adams restored order and he and I convinced the rest of the owners to meet the next day, go on with the draft, select an eighth franchise to be named later, and get around to selecting a commissioner. Then we adjourned.

We had met with high hopes and left with our chins on the floor. The Minneapolis group played us for fools. As it turned out, they even succeeded in getting their man, Joe Foss, elected commissioner. My choice for the league's top job was Frank Leahy, but the Minnesota group and Hunt voted him down. I then recommended Edward "Moose" Krause, and Krause sat well with everybody. But Moose turned us down because he didn't want to leave Notre Dame where he had been Athletic Director for so many years and where he and his family had many ties. My third choice, Rip Miller, athletic director at the Naval Academy, was also turned down by Hunt and Skoglund. (Yes, Boyer and Skoglund were still at the meeting.) Then Hunt and Skoglund decided to try to hire H.O. "Fritz" Crisler away from Michigan University. Crisler asked for $100,000 a year for five years and a fat insurance policy. We turned him down. The offer to Crisler was ridiculous anyway. He had for years publicly stated that pro football was inferior to college ball and had opposed the pros at every opportunity. Having him would have been a kiss of death. Our final choice wasn't much better, for me, as it turned out.

Foss was the only candidate left. He had first been recommended by the Minneapolis group at the Beverly Hills meeting in September, with mine being the only negative vote. I had nothing against Foss as a person. He had been a great war hero and then governor of South Dakota, but he didn't know anything about football, had no experience and few contacts in the game, and if we were going to stand a chance against the NFL, we needed a football man, one experienced in the ways of rough and tumble in-fighting. Foss didn't have the qualities necessary to lead us then and, to my way of thinking, he still doesn't. When he was proposed for commissioner, Foss was in Skoglund's employ as vice-president of Raven Industries, an outfit making balloons for aerial research. In 1964, *Who's Who in America* still listed Foss as a Raven director. Football, too, sometimes makes strange bed-fellows.

After Foss was elected, the owners asked me to help select an assistant commissioner. I picked Milt Woodard, former newspaperman and director of the Western Golf Association. Milt accepted and we had a first-rate backup man for the commissioner.

The next day we held our draft. Boyer and Skoglund were still insisting that they wanted to join the AFL and carry on, but I knew that was sheer malarkey and insisted that they be kept out. My rather timid and naïve colleagues overruled me.

The gimmick in the Minneapolis situation was Met Stadium, built by private capital but run by a municipal commission. Johnson, whose paper had contributed heavily to the building of the stadium, had a great deal to say about its disposition. There was no doubt, in all that Johnson did, that it would be the NFL that would play in Met Stadium if he had anything to do with it. Skoglund, Winter, and Boyer had no contract of any sort for use of the stadium. Later, when they were quite sure that the NFL was coming in, they used the stadium board as an excuse to withdraw from the AFL. The board, Boyer reported, would not approve the AFL tenant until it became known whether there would be an NFL franchise. Thereupon, Minneapolis officially withdrew on December 30, 1959, from the AFL.

On January 18, Boyer was in the other league, making a formal presentation for an NFL franchise. It was granted, with Boyer, Winter, and Skoglund holding 20 percent apiece; B.H. Ridder, Jr., St. Paul publisher, 30 percent, and Oluf Haugsrud of Duluth, 10 percent.

Looking back, the Minneapolis group wanted an NFL franchise and if they couldn't get one, then the AFL would do.
They played us against the NFL and won. They were the tool
George Halas and the NFL used to cripple us. Halas almost
succeeded in making us quit before we began. Halas plays
rough, and if Adams, Wilson, and I hadn't fought back that
night, he would have won. As it was, he eliminated the AFL
from the Midwest, and until the league gets a franchise in
football's heartland, it will never approach the NFL in popularity or prestige.

Filling out the league with an eighth franchise was our para-
mount problem as we approached the meeting at Dallas,
January 26, 1960. After the walkout of the Minnesota crowd,
the new franchise would have very little time to organize and
would undoubtedly be handicapped.

Barron Hilton fought successfully for the admission of Oakland, California, even though the city did not have a stadium
and had to play in San Francisco for two years. We had to go
along with Hilton, although the situation in Oakland was far
from encouraging. It was the first stiff penalty we paid for the
NFL raid that took Minneapolis from us. It might have been
better to have restored our hold on the Midwest, but with only
eight teams it was difficult to try to cover the entire country.

Oakland got a desperately raw deal coming into the league.
Charles "Chet" Soda, a construction man who originally headed
the syndicate, was tossed the Minneapolis draft list from the
preceding November 22, and told it was his. That's all there
was; there wasn't any more. He soon learned that most of the
players assigned to him had signed with the NFL, or with other
AFL clubs, inasmuch as for two months they had no club to
deal with. Eddie Erdelatz, a fine coach, took the sweepings and
stunned the league by winning 6 of his 14 games the first
season, but in the end the scarcity of talent ruined his long,
honorable career. His pleas for a fair break at the meetings
were resented by some, mainly Hunt, who failed to understand

the importance of making each team as competitive as possible. I supported the Oakland group and remember telling Foss that he should support Oakland and try to get the other owners to help. As usual, he ignored my suggestion. The next season, Oakland opened by losing 55-0 to Houston and 44-0 to San Diego. Erdelatz was fired. The team won only two games that year and on November 5, 1961, it began the longest losing streak in pro football history, 19 straight. The team became a joke, but it wasn't until August, 1962, that the league helped with a special draft for Oakland and Denver. My suggestion to Foss was finally implemented.

One novelty that came out of the Dallas meeting was our adoption of the college option rule permitting either a one-point placement kick or a two-point run or pass play after touchdowns. It was my proposal, but it was adopted only over the strong objection of some of the owners, particularly Ralph Wilson, who felt we would be accused of copying the colleges. At that point we might have adjourned, had not Lamar Hunt dropped a bombshell into the meeting. He was, he informed us, going to sue the NFL for $10 million, asking treble damages, or $30 million, under the antitrust code, because he felt they had been guilty of monopoly and conspiracy in knocking us off in Minneapolis and in entering Dallas. I was dumbfounded, but the rest of the members thought Hunt had a good idea. At least, they were going along with him. But I fought Hunt bitterly and pleaded with him to get a sound outside legal opinion. He agreed to listen to my lawyer in Washington, Clark Clifford, an expert on antitrust.

When I called Clifford from Dallas, he left the dinner table and talked to our members for more than an hour. All of us listened, including Foss. Clifford explained patiently and at length that we had no case. In view of the fact that we had teams in New York and Los Angeles, which also were NFL cities, we could hardly allege a monopoly. Don't think I would have turned down $30 million from the NFL. What gnawed at me was the conviction that we were setting up a smashing victory for the NFL. That didn't deter Hunt, and with Foss now trailing behind like a kite, he insisted on filing a complaint with the Department of Justice, which apparently saw no basis for prosecution. In any event, Hunt & Foss started their civil suit.

When I heard that Hunt and his legal beagles had decided to file suit in Baltimore, I was sure he would lose and begged him to switch. The politics of the thing were obvious. Carroll Rosenbloom, owner of the Colts, was as close to Joe Kennedy as anyone in the country. And in Washington, sitting on the desk of Attorney General Robert F. Kennedy, was the football, autographed by the 1958 Colts, from the "greatest game ever played." It was given to Kennedy by his close friend, Carroll Rosenbloom. But Warren E. Baker, the Washington lawyer Foss brought in, said it would make no difference filing in Baltimore.

Hunt did not sue the Minnesota Vikings because they had not been in existence at the time of the alleged wrongs, and he had to excuse San Francisco and Los Angeles at the outset because he had little presumed evidence against them. Nor did he include Washington in the suit, for Marshall had repeated to Hunt and his lawyer what he had said publicly, that "the only reason for expansion I have heard from other owners is that we would destroy the new league."

Hunt's suit contended that all the NFL defendants had monopolized major league football and that all except the Washington Redskins had attempted to monopolize and conspired to monopolize metropolitan areas that were essential to the success of professional football franchises. Our lawyers argued that the granting of NFL franchises to Dallas and to Minneapolis, and statements made with respect to a proposed franchise for Houston, constituted an "exercise of monopoly power," and that those acts were carried out as part of a plot.

The NFL counsel denied that his league had monopoly power, pointing out that the AFL had entered New York City and Los Angeles, and that the questioned franchises were granted, and statements about expansion into Houston were made, according to a well-publicized plan of expansion adopted before there had been a second league.

Since pro football existed only in leagues, and not as separate clubs, the test of monopoly power in our case was whether the NFL had sufficient power to prevent the formation or successful operation of a new league. It wouldn't suffice, Judge Roszel Thomsen ruled at the outset, to show that the NFL had the power to bar another league from any one city or group of cities unless that act frustrated the formation of the league. Intent was not necessary to prove monopoly; the act of excluding competitors was enough, even if unintentional.

Judge Thomsen went on to point out that an intent to exclude competitors from only a part of the market was not sufficient to prove conspiracy, unless the partial ban would drive a rival out of the entire market. Hunt's lawyers contended that the NFL plotted to drive the AFL out of Dallas and Minneapolis in the belief that the loss of these two cities would make it impossible for the new league to operate at all.

As the trial developed, Hunt's case for conspiracy was seen to rely almost exclusively on Marshall's statement. However, this stand became untenable when Judge Thomsen noted that Marshall's quoted statement was not true because he (Marshall) had heard many different reasons for expansion from the NFL owners.

Before filing the suit, Hunt had sent his attorney, and sometimes had accompanied him, on visits to various NFL owners, apparently to try to collect information that could be used in the case. About these activities, the justice observed: "It is remarkable—and characteristic—how many of the owners were willing to talk to Hunt's attorney without having their own attorneys present. The court does not accept all of the testimony of Hunt's attorney with respect to what was told him, but finds that the NFL owners generally stated their differing view with respect to expansion." Judge Thomsen emphasized that "there was no evidence" that NFL representatives at any time were not candid in the statements they made to Hunt, or that they gave him any advice which they did not believe to be sound. On the contrary, the justice pointed out, they gave Hunt much sound advice, and even revealed to him how the NFL operated. Contrariwise, Thomsen added that Hunt by his own admission had been secretive and devious in his methods, and had hidden his plans from the NFL men.

Oddly enough, the success of the NFL franchise in Minneapolis was strongly offered by Hunt's attorneys as evidence that the AFL had been harmed. However, the court felt that an AFL team would not have had comparable success, and for many reasons. The Minnesota Vikings began operating with experienced professional management, it had many well-known professional players from established clubs, and the stadium commission was willing to enlarge seating capacity from 22,000 to 40,000. None of these factors, the court believed, would have attended an AFL franchise. In fact, it was doubtful whether all of the three AFL franchises really intended to go ahead with their franchise, the report of the suit related. At the time of the November telegrams and meeting, they had no general manager or coach, no stadium lease, and no significant business commitment.

In reviewing the case, Judge Thomsen brought in the AFL "fact book" and noted that it stated "never before in the history of sports has a sports organization gone so far so fast." Then why sue? It was also brought out during the suit that Hunt had approached Bell and others in an attempt to arrive at a common player draft and to establish common television blackouts. The court noted that both proposals were of doubtful validity, at best.

On the question of monopoly the justice ruled that the plaintiffs had failed to show any lack of sufficient qualified applicants for franchises, and that the NFL obviously did not control this market. It was also proved that while the NFL might drive the AFL out of one city, it never intended to go into every AFL city, nor even expand above the limit of sixteen clubs. This point destroyed Hunt's and Foss' claim that the NFL could add enough new cities to overwhelm the AFL. Inasmuch as the AFL went into business and continued in business, the NFL did not have monopoly power and was cleared by the court of that charge.

Now Foss' lawyers had to rely on the claim of conspiracy and to show that some acts were undertaken with the specific intent of destroying the rival league. The court held that the AFL had failed to show any motive behind NFL actions that could be deemed illegal. The Texas territory, for example, had long been considered desirable, and the move to Minneapolis was made only after Houston was unavailable. The overall strategy of the NFL was consistent with its long-range plans, the court ruled, and in line with reasonable competitive business methods to guard an enterprise against a rival.

There was a parting shot at Hunt which intimated that even if the NFL had been found in violation on any count, the damages due the plaintiff might not be considerable. The court phrased the thought in these words: "Hunt and many of the other AFL owners were eager to become a part of the alleged monopoly, and also proposed to the NFL that they join in agreements of doubtful validity to keep down the amounts they would have to pay the players and to place restrictions on telecasting. Those acts of Hunt and other AFL owners would not prevent recourse . . . although they might properly be considered in determining the equitable relief

which might be granted if defendants were guilty of any violation of the laws which would render them liable to plaintiffs."

In his decision on May 21, 1962, Judge Thomsen rendered
these verdicts: "Neither individually nor in concert have the
defendants monopolized any part of the trade or commerce
among the several states; particularly they have not monopolized major league professional football.

"None of the defendants has engaged in a combination or
conspiracy in unreasonable restraint of trade or commerce
among the several states in the presentation of major league
professional football games.

"None of the plaintiffs is entitled to relief in this case against
the defendants.

"Judgment will be entered in favor of the defendants, with
costs."

The word "costs" really hurts when you drop a case, and in
this instance, it was ironic.

Clark Clifford, one of the nation's outstanding lawyers, gave
the AFL the right advice for nothing, yet Hunt and Foss went
ahead and soaked each franchise about $50,000 in legal fees
to arrive at exactly the same conclusion. That was quite a load
of hay to lay on a struggling franchise; I wouldn't have minded
so much if I had a rich father.

We were wrong to sue the NFL. We had no case, but under
the ineffective leadership of Hunt and Foss we were able to
make ourselves look ridiculous and in addition each to drop
$50,000. Hindsight is easier than foresight, but we were told
beforehand we would lose, and we did.

The AFL publishes an *Official Guide* and in it there is a
section of so-called "Historical Highlights." History to me
means fact, or as close to fact as study and research can come.
This *Guide,* then, is the League's fact book. In the fact book
there is an item reading: "Package TV—Cooperative television

plan adopted whereby league office negotiates television contract, proceeds from which are divided equally among member
clubs." Sounds simple. Almost as if Joe Foss called ABC and
said, "let's televise our games." It wasn't easy; nor did anybody
in the AFL "adopt" this television package. It was handed to
them because of my connections, my knowledge, my work, and
my money. It is the Wismer Plan. It was new to pro football.
The NFL "adopted" it later, but it was original with the AFL.

There are organizations that like to make up their own history, but I just thought somebody in the AFL might have given
me a credit line, at least, for the $2 million I fed the league.
The history of the television package is easy to relate; I was
there from start to finish.

Today, in pro sports, payroll and overhead costs are so
tremendous that a franchise either has a lucrative television
contract or it isn't in business at all. That's why I got right to
work on the television detail after the disaster at Minneapolis
—we needed a morale-builder fast. We didn't have an eighth
team. We had hired only a few coaches and players. Everyone
was anxious and uneasy.

I already had talked to several people about radio and TV
rights for my team, the Titans. I could have sold locally, like
baseball, and probably received $400,000 for all 14 games, in-
cluding home contests, because not many fans were going to
be enticed to the ramshackle old Polo Grounds. In that event,
however, Denver would receive only $35,000, Dallas maybe
$65,000, Houston $70,000, and so on. Then we would have
had a situation similar to the one in baseball, where the
Yankees control but do not share the richest television market
in the country, while the rest of the American League must
get along on less.

We didn't have an established league. We had to launch
one. Everybody had to get some money, or one or two clubs
would prosper for a time and then the league would fail. This

wasn't new and original thinking on my part; that was part of
the philosophy I had formed from my NFL days, something
I had learned from Richards, from Marshall, and from Bell.

Harry Haggerty was a close friend of mine from Notre Dame
days. He was not an alumnus of Notre Dame, but he was on
the advisory council of the university. He was also the man
in charge of lending money for the Metropolitan Life Insurance
Company. Haggerty listened to my story and with his combination of intimate football knowledge and shrewd business sense,
he concluded that we might have a chance. We had an un-
known league, but the product, pro football, was very popular.
We were national, with a hold in the two great markets of
New York and Los Angeles, so that the wealthy sponsors might
be interested. Haggerty said he would carry the ball and
arrange a meeting with ABC executives. In these dealings I
acted as chairman of the AFL Television Committee. I invited
Lamar Hunt to the Haggerty meetings.

Ollie Trays, president of ABC, and Leonard Goldenson,
chairman of the board, were there with Haggerty, who had
me present my proposition. They agreed on the proposal to go
on the air in 1960—if I or someone I selected—could sell 50
percent of the time. On rough figuring, half of the package
would mean over $2 million to be put up by sponsors. I spent
at least $50,000 of my own money, entertaining advertising
executives and potential sponsors, to put the deal across, and
never asked the league to reimburse me. I was willing to spend
the money because I knew I was breathing life into the young
league. Most of my help came from the Young and Rubicam
Ad Agency. General Cigar was the first sponsor. Then we
signed Sinclair Oil and were over the mark.

The gentlemen who put up the $2 million accepted us on
good faith, because we did not have a product to show, nor
even a full team as yet. Not a uniform had been issued, nor a
cleat worn. The Wismer Plan gave the league a chance. It may

be that some of our members didn't need the money, but they certainly didn't show any signs of generosity when I was going under and needed help. They had not learned, as the NFL owners had, to protect their own.

I went the limit to cooperate with our television policy by letting outside games be telecast into New York when my Titans were playing at the Polo Grounds. Milt Woodard, assistant commissioner, would make the request because sponsors were screaming for exposure in the New York market. Permitting the telecasting of outside games probably didn't hurt our gate very much, but I could have refused Woodard's requests, kept the New York market for myself, and let the rest of the league shift for itself. That was the kind of response I would later receive from the league when I needed help.

When the NFL adopted the Wismer Plan in April, 1962, Judge Allan K. Grim of the U.S. District Court voided the package deal made with CBS. The owners presumably had ignored Grim's injunction of 1953, which forbade them to act together on a contract because the judge deemed it an unfair restriction on the television business. The AFL was not under injunction, and the Justice Department didn't object, so we went ahead. The NFL moved within the law when Congress passed a bill permitting pro leagues to make one-network deals.

We were promised $1,785,000 by ABC for our first season, 1960, which would mean almost $225,000 a club. I say "promised" because that is what most sponsored television packages are, *promises*. If the network sells so much air space to sponsors, the contract says, the league will receive so much money. Then there are loopholes and escape clauses to scale down league revenue if the space is sold only in part, or at cut rates.

The attractiveness and desirability of the event, or sport, is what will determine the proceeds. When CBS bid $14.1 million per year for rights to NFL games in 1964 and 1965, there wasn't much doubt that the price would come out right for the old pros, because they were extravagantly popular with sponsors. Under the terms of the NBC-AFL agreement for $35 million in "if" money over five years, beginning in 1965, the amounts that the clubs in the new league actually receive from year to year will be a measure of their value as sponsors see them. The more popular the clubs are, the nearer the league will come to the $35-million mark.

In round figures, each AFL Club drew $200,000 in 1960, when I sold half the package for ABC. In 1961, Barron Hilton brought in David A. "Sonny" Werblin, then of MCA, as our agent, and with 10 percent off for MCA fees, the amount dropped to $165,000. It went up to $190,000 in 1962, to $200,000 in 1963, and was negligible, say $75,000 to $100,000 in 1964, as the ABC contract ran out.

Lining up a coach for the Titans proved to be a tougher job than I had anticipated. It was, of course, difficult to persuade a man in an established position to quit and take a chance, because nobody could offer any assurance on the length of time the AFL might stay in business. I offered Duffy Daugherty a fabulous deal, $25,000 a year for 5 years, in 1960 to leave Michigan State. Duffy took my proposition in to John Hanna, president of the university, and came out of the negotiations with a big raise. Dick Gallagher, now general manager of the Buffalo Bills and former coach at Santa Clara, also was on my list, but Ralph Wilson got to him first.

Otto Graham, the great quarterback of the Browns from 1946 through 1955, seemed interested in the Titans until he talked it over with his wife. Mrs. Graham objected to Otto's taking to the road again and he respected her wishes.

One Sunday afternoon at Deepdale Golf Club, I was trying to amass another list of candidates when my man flashed on the television screen, Sammy Baugh. Sam was being interviewed at half time of the Giants-Redskins game in Wash-

ington. I phoned the press box in D.C. and as soon as Sam was
finished with the interview, he was talking to me. I told Sam
I had a deal I thought he'd like, filled him in on the new league,
and asked him to come to New York to see me. Sam had to
come to New York anyway to get a plane back to Texas so he
agreed to talk. We met the next morning about 9 A.M. at Idlewild. We sat on a bench outside the Brass Rail restaurant, had
a cigar, and talked. It had to be quick because Sam's flight left
at 9:55 A.M., so I laid the story out for him, stressing the promi-
nence of Texans in the league. He knew these people, knew me,
and thought the league had a chance, especially with TV. We
walked to the plane and Sam and I shook hands. He agreed
to coach the New York Titans.

We held a gala press conference a few days later in New
York to announce Baugh's signing, and the incident drew headlines all over the country—in Washington, Chicago, Texas, and
in New York. The Baugh signing was the first big sensational
publicity story of the AFL, and it remained the headline champion until Joe Namath went for $400,000.

Sam's salary was $28,000 and before he would meet the
press, Sam wanted to be paid. The party was in my apartment
so Sam, Joe Arcuni, and I retired to my bedroom. Arcuni, who
had made his fortune in the dressmaking business, had been
recommended to me by Bill Shea as a possible partner. He
came into the Titans for 10 percent of the club. He always
carried a big roll and paid Sam on the spot. Joe counted out
$28,000 in cash and laid it out before Sam. Baugh picked it up,
stuffed it in his pocket, and signed the contract. Then we all
went out to meet the sports press.

Sam and I didn't always get along. I certainly needed and
demanded top effort, but Sam disliked putting any discipline
into coaching. The players liked him and he liked them, but
that wasn't giving me 100 percent. Baugh felt that the players
were pros and required very little supervision to keep them-

selves in shape and ready to go at top speed. That is the way
Sam himself was, but not all of the players he had in his charge
followed their coach's example. I remember one in particular,
a college star who had been drafted by the NFL and by us.
We signed him and thought we had a real find. He was 6'3",
245 lbs., and a good tackle in college. We switched him to
guard and eagerly awaited the results. Well, he turned out to
be a "quittin' Steve." He didn't put out in practice or in the
game, didn't stay in shape, and was a bad influence on the club.
I've often thought that if Sam had cracked down on him he
may have straightened him out and made him into the player
his potential indicated he was. Maybe he thought he didn't
have to put out. After all, some of those guys thought the AFL
was minor league and they could make any team without trying. Well, most of those bums are out of the league now. They
didn't have the guts to take their chance in the NFL, came
over to the AFL looking for a free ride, and couldn't understand
when I or some other owner expected them to put out. Today,
there is little of that in the AFL.

Baugh used good judgment in picking his assistants, and he
had full say in the matter. He chose George Sauer, Bones
Taylor, Dick Todd, and John Steber. Only Sauer is still with
the team. Taylor switched jobs with Sam at Houston, with
Bones top man and Baugh his aide. Todd was a fine football
man but retired, and Steber had been an assistant of Sam's
at Hardin-Simmons.

Despite the bumps along the road, Baugh and I parted as
friends. In 1962, I replaced Sammy during his third year with
"Bulldog" Turner, the former Bear great.

When Sam became head coach of the Houston Oilers in
1964, I phoned my congratulations. He gave me a play-by-play
account of the signing.

"They asked me how you and me finished up," Sam related,
"and I said we finished up the best of friends. They wanted

to know whether I got paid and I told them sure I got paid."
Then Baugh informed me that the press wanted to know why
the Titans had failed. "They just ran out of money," was
Baugh's typical laconic reply.

I was lucky to find a general manager. To put it another
way, Steve Sebo was unlucky. He was fired by the University
of Pennsylvania in one of those typical factional tiffs in college
football, just after he had coached the Quakers to the Ivy
League title in 1959. I hired him and again got headlines.
Steve came from Battle Creek, Michigan, and was a classmate
and teammate of mine at Michigan State. He had coached at
Michigan and Harvard before becoming head man at Penn.
He was a popular coach as well as a talented one, and the
sentimental overtones of his situation ushered him into the pros
on a wave of publicity. Penn hasn't done well since he left.
Both Baugh and Sebo made as much money with me as any
others in similar positions in the AFL.

As for money of any color but my own, I found very little.
Bill Shea, who had led me to believe he was going to rush in
financial reinforcements, delivered just once, when he introduced me to Joe Arcuni. Joe didn't stay around very long.
After our opening exhibition-game loss to the Chargers, Joe
decided to take his $45,000 and pull out, and with him went
all Bill Shea's connections with the Titans. Bill didn't leave
much of an impression on the game. Not including Arcuni's
money, the total outside support for the Titans amounted to
$110,000. If it had been a million and ten I might have had a
chance.

We had to build a roster and build it in a hurry. We were
under a handicap signing players because I began to realize
at this point that there would be no flow of money from New
York City or from Bill Shea and his contacts. Without it, I was
not able to block out, say, $300,000 to use in bidding for some
top-name players. This explanation is given in fairness to Sebo,

who worked quietly and hard, was popular with the players, coaches, and press, and achieved excellent results. He did not have *carte blanche* nor a couple of oil wells to toss into the kitty for stars, as he might have had at Houston or Dallas, but he put together an interesting team and came up with many players who still remain with the Jets or have been passed on to other clubs in the league.

From our clean, sunny, New Hampshire camp we were scheduled to make our league debut in the shabby, desolate Polo Grounds, which had been deteriorating steadily since the New York baseball Giants moved to San Francisco for the 1958 season. A soccer league had played on the "pitch," but that merely aggravated conditions for football. The stands and seats were encrusted with grime. There was not enough parking space to matter. The neighborhood was not good. In brief, this was the worst possible place to attract paying customers.

The *New York Daily News* ran pictures of the sorry state of the Polo Grounds, but the Giants, who held the lease, were unmoved. Horace Stoneham, Giant president, probably had no love for football. He suffered a severe financial blow when he failed to prevent the football Giants from moving across the Harlem River to Yankee Stadium in 1956. The football team was at its peak; it brought in revenue. The loss of that revenue helped put Stoneham in a financial squeeze that led him to San Francisco. The move of the Giants to Yankee Stadium was one of the turning points in the history of sports.

Without football, Stoneham was vulnerable. Had he persuaded the football Giants to string along with him, the two could have had the Flushing stadium built much earlier. Stoneham might have kept the football Giants by appealing to the late Tim Mara, founder, who probably would have complied. It was Bert Bell, NFL commissioner, who insisted on a Yankee Stadium deal when the league could not obtain assurances that Stoneham would remain in the city. When the football Giants crossed the river to Yankeeville, their advance ticket sale went up 50 percent. And I was stuck with the musty, decaying stadium they were fleeing from.

I dealt with Edgar P. Feeley, secretary and attorney for the Stoneham interests in New York. The lease was held by the National Exhibition Company (Stoneham), to which I agreed to pay a minimum of $7,500 per game or 13 percent of the gate after taxes. All I received in turn was use of the park—no concessions, no parking, no service. Feeley shrugged off the condition of the field and told me it would have to do. Restoring it to decent shape cost me $15,000.

Our season began under an ill star and was fated to continue that way.

Our opening in the Polo Grounds was on September 11 against the Buffalo Bills. The night of September 10 was lovely, with the temperature around 75° and I thought we might at least get a break from the weather. By 8 A.M. on the eleventh, the wind had shifted and Hurricane Diana was bearing down on the city. As gametime approached, the weather worsened steadily and we were forced to play in rain and hail driven by a wind that at times reached 70 mph in gusts. It was the most wretched day for football in my memory, and we didn't draw more than 7,500 paid. Since I had first met with Lamar Hunt, I had looked forward to this night. My disappointment at the weather was forgotten as I watched my team dressing in the locker room. Their jerseys were dark blue with gold lettering, pants of gold with dark blue stripes down the legs, helmets of gold, and stockings of blue with thin gold stripes. As I walked around the room chatting with the players, my feelings were obvious. This was my team, wearing my colors, the colors made famous by Notre Dame, and not even Hurricane Diana could ruin that moment for me. Pride—I was bursting with it.

We did get a good competitive start. In the locker room before the game I told the players that I was aware of the difficult conditions they would face. I promised them a bonus of $2,500 a man if they won the Eastern Division title, and one of $5,000 should they take the league championship. They responded with a 27-3 decision over the Bills and presented me with the game ball, one of the prized mementos of my life.

Joe Foss and I almost staged an unscheduled fight one night at 21, the plush New York restaurant which has been the scene of a number of bouts that didn't quite make the marquee at Madison Square Garden. The AFL commissioner and I had no particular grudge against each other when we entered the club. David A. "Sonny" Werblin was our host. Barron Hilton had just brought in the MCA representative to be our television agent, and Sonny was celebrating. After dinner we milled around the bar in approved 21 fashion and I found myself next to Werblin. I told him how lucky he was to be stepping into a contract that took me two years of my own time and money to line up. The MCA man didn't seem to like my re-marks, although it was true that he was going to get a fee for a contract that had been made in 1960 on a five-year basis.

Werblin retorted that he would get the contract and my team as well. I turned to Foss and asked him if Werblin was there to steal my team. Foss replied haughtily that I couldn't talk to him that way and threatened to beat me up. I began calling his bluff, but other hands intervened and we were separated. I must say, though, Werblin was a prophetic guy. He was taking my measure as early as the spring of 1961. At the same time, Foss' attitude was typical. Whenever there was a chance to oppose me, he seized it, although he was taking my money to represent me as commissioner, along with that of seven other members. That didn't seem to bother Foss.

Werblin came into the league from show business. He is a native of Brooklyn who attended Rutgers University and was

employed by Music Corporation of America until he was let
go last winter. He also is a stockholder in the Monmouth Race
Track in New Jersey, where the AFL meetings were held
this year. Whether or not Joe Namath plays well for the Jets,
I estimate that Werblin got at least $400,000 worth of personal
publicity out of the deal for the Alabama quarterback. One
New York paper called Werblin the Ziegfeld of Football, although he has yet to put on any kind of major league football
production and fields a lackluster team.

I was somewhat puzzled by the way Werblin would be
identified as "the owner" of the Jets practically every time he
was interviewed. It had been my understanding that I sold
my franchise to a group of five persons, including Werblin.
At lunch one day I met Townsend Martin, banker and socialite,
whom I had thought to be a member of the Jets' syndicate, and
I inquired of him just who did own the Jets. Martin promptly
replied that he, Leon Hess, and Werblin held equal shares
and that Don Lillis and Phil Islin had lesser shares. Finally,
I had it straight. Lillis is a stockbroker; Hess, an oil man, and
Islin, an executive of the Monmouth track.

The way I saw it, as the '61 season approached, the AFL
had better catch on with the public in a hurry, or I would run
out of ready cash. The Flushing stadium was behind schedule
and we faced the bleak prospect of having to return to the
Polo Grounds. We had not drawn as much as 100,000 paid in
our first year and could not expect much better in the second
season, even with an honest count by the gate-keepers. Advance
ticket sales at home were discouragingly slow and things looked
gloomier on the road. On a three-game Western trip to Denver,
Oakland, and Los Angeles in 1960, with an entourage of 55
to 60 persons, my losses were close to $150,000. All that came
in was the guarantee of $20,000 in each city, or a total of
$60,000, which did not begin to cover overall expenses.

As short of fans as we were in the Polo Grounds, the worst

sight I saw that first season was the Coliseum at Los Angeles. In this vast bowl which has a capacity of over 100,000 people, the Chargers drew three or four thousand. The Coliseum at Los Angeles looked like a sterile slide under a microscope. Oakland's Raiders attracted nobody because they were playing in San Francisco and San Franciscans look on Oakland the way New Yorkers regard Bridgeport.

In 56 games in 1960, four games rewarded visiting teams with more than the guarantee of $20,000. Two were in Buffalo and two in Boston, and the total payment over the guarantees in the four games was only $7,250. We had nobody to lean on in the AFL in our early years, but the NFL did. For example, in the NFL the St. Louis Cardinals drew only 129,174 to tiny Busch Stadium in 1962, but they played to 335,000 on their seven road dates. They received 40 percent of the net receipts on the road to cover their home deficits.

In our case, through the 1960-62 period, we were merely exchanging the same old weary $20,000 guarantee. Nobody could help anyone else. Last year, with Shea Stadium such a glittering new attraction, the Jets were able to help the rest of the AFL.

The Jets, for example, could give the Broncos a check for $56,000, representing 40 percent of the net receipts. Then, when the Jets played in Denver to a small crowd, the Broncos would not have to dig up fresh money for the guarantee, which had been raised to $30,000. They merely passed back $30,000 of the $56,000 they had received in New York.

That sort of support has been going on in the NFL for years. A team doing badly at home can get well on the road in that league, or at least avert disaster, because of the sizable visitor's share from big gates on the road. The Pittsburgh Steelers in 1962 actually put more money in their pocket for their seven road games than for the seven they played at home in Forbes Field and Pitt Stadium.

For 1965 the AFL hopes to have three very strong "payoff" cities—Houston, Buffalo, with enlarged facilities, and New York. Boston could become a fourth. For 1966 Oakland promised to have a new stadium ready that might attract more fans.

The lack of gate-attraction stars, particularly glittering new quarterbacks, cramped the AFL through its first five years and is bound to hurt for some years to come. The Jets made money at home because of their new stadium, but their mediocre team compiled a dreadful record on the road. In 1964 the Jets drew 11,309 in Denver, 15,589 in Oakland, and only 22,716 in Boston, where they might have established a natural rivalry with the Patriots. The Patriots found their real rival in Buffalo.

It is interesting to notice that the NFL had some soft spots as recently as 1958; that is how fast pro football has galloped on. In 1958 the Cardinals, then playing in Chicago, drew only 95,000 paid for six games in Comiskey Park, and NFL fans were almost equally discriminating in other cities. The New York Giants drew 71,000 for Baltimore in Yankee Stadium (capacity now is limited to 63,000), yet pulled only 25,000 at Pittsburgh and 33,000 at Philadelphia. Before Vince Lombardi exerted his magic, Milwaukee was lukewarm toward the Green Bay Packers, who drew only 18,000 for a game with the San Francisco 49ers. The 49ers, although quite popular in Kezar Stadium, drew only 18,000 in St. Louis and 23,000 in Philadelphia. Pittsburgh was far from being a firm box-office franchise, and Detroit and Cleveland, usually strong at the gate, suffered slumps depending on the visiting attraction.

The 1961 season was a dreary repetition of 1960 at the gate, although Baugh's team played highly exciting football and ended the season, as it had the year before, with 7 games won and 7 games lost.

We were laying the groundwork for the AFL in those early years and taking the losses while the league became known,

but the operation was too costly for me. As 1961 closed I had
to have help to underwrite a third season. I had given up hope
of assistance from the New York politicians, including Bill
Shea, and I was getting the impression there would be no helping hand extended by my associates in the AFL. When I approached them, they turned me down flat. They were not
interested.

Why should they help me? I was naïve enough to think
there were two reasons. First, Lamar Hunt had looked to me
for help when he wanted to start the league, and I thought he
might tide me over a season with the loan of a million or so,
a loan that he never would have missed. Bud Adams too was
immensely wealthy, and frankly, he disappointed me. Second,
my background had led me to believe that partners in a league
help one another. Unfortunately, that was strictly NFL thinking. It had not entered the television league.

I was close to Bert Bell when he was NFL commissioner and
knew his solicitude for the weaker franchises. He put a shield
in front of the Green Bay Packers in their dark days, and
protected any club that was down, including the mighty New
York Giants on several occasions.

When Ted Collins left the league after eight straight money-
losing seasons, in 1952, he was not forced out. I know because
George Marshall represented the league in dealing with Collins
and I was there with Marshall. Collins had lost for five years
in Boston from 1944–48. Then in 1949 he took an awful socking
when he shared the Polo Grounds with the Giants in fighting
the Yankees of the All America Football Conference. Finally,
he played in Yankee Stadium from 1950–51 but could not stand
bucking the Giants just across the Harlem River.

Marshall explained to Collins that Bell and the owners most
likely would authorize moving the franchise to Dallas if he
resigned. However, Marshall stressed, why shouldn't Collins
go down into that new territory and try to establish himself.

It was up to Ted; the league would see that he could carry on.

Collins was too much of a New Yorker to go all the way to Texas; for him even Boston was too far removed. When Collins definitely withdrew, Marshall was empowered and prepared to handle all details. The league would give Collins $100,000 for his franchise, and the league would pay off his lease on Yankee Stadium, which still had eight years to run at a guarantee of $25,000 yearly. The Giants would cancel the sum still owed to them for sharing their territory with him.

That was a friendly, generous deal all the way. Then there was the Danny Reeves case, which in some ways was similar to mine. Reeves in December of 1962 was able to regain control of the Los Angeles Rams, the club he took west from Cleveland in 1946, but he probably would have been squeezed out if Bell had not protected his interests.

Reeves in 1947 needed more operating capital to fight Ben Lindheimer's Los Angeles Dons of the AAFC, and got it by offering shares in the Rams to sportsmen who would help him pay the bills. That is, Reeves would give you 30 percent of the club if you paid 30 percent of the bills. In that way, Edwin and Harold Pauley, Fred Levy, Jr., Hal Seley, and Bob Hope joined Reeves.

Reeves whittled his own holdings down to one-third of the franchise, and his position was anything but secure when his partners began differing with him in the early Fifties, when the Rams held Los Angeles exclusively.

Ed Pauley, an oil tycoon who can afford to donate millions to charity each year, headed the opposition. The discordant partners went to court and the club was immobilized, with no one in command. Bell ran it from Philadelphia through Tex Schramm, now general manager of the Dallas Cowboys, and Pete Rozelle, now NFL commissioner.

Bell protected Reeves from the tremendous financial pressure being mounted against him. At league meetings the commissioner would not recognize any of the partners but Reeves. Bell would rule: "Reeves is the president of record and he speaks for the Los Angeles club." I can well imagine that Bell remembered when he was in the same position as Reeves, and how George Halas and others had picked him up.

In 1962 Reeves obtained reinforcements. Gene Autry, Robert O. Reynolds, and Leonard K. Firestone of the Los Angeles Angels baseball syndicate joined him for a showdown with Ed Pauley. Paul O'Bryan of Washington, D.C., brought the group together.

When Pauley came to the Rams in 1947 he bought 30 percent of the franchise for $1 million, on the proviso that he would share losses at 30¢ on the dollar. He told me he lost about $160,000 in the first four years, but netted about $300,000 from 1951 on. For the showdown, Pauley represented two-thirds of the club and Reeves one-third. They agreed to present simultaneous bids based on the total value of the club, and the winner would pay the loser his share in cash. That is, if Pauley won he would give Reeves one-third of the price he had bid, and if Reeves was high man he would turn over to Pauley two-thirds of the amount he had offered.

There was one more rule that distinguished this auction. It was not going to be a penny-ante affair. The low man always would have the privilege of bidding again, provided he topped the high offer by at least 20 percent. That was stiff.

The Pauley faction was knocked out in the first round. Pauley priced the Rams at $6.1 million. Reeves' figure was an astonishing $7.1 million. Then, if Pauley cared to bid again, he would have had to top Reeves by 20 percent, which meant $8.5 million. Pauley resigned; he was not prepared to bid more than $7 million and he would not let his vanity overcome his common sense. The money was not a factor; to him $8.5 million was simply the price of another luxury.

I used the Reeves approach to potential investors as a last

resort in 1962. Pay my debts in exchange for a piece of the club, was the idea, and it was expanded to offer control of the franchise to anyone who would guarantee 75 percent of the club on that basis, while retaining only 25 percent.

Earlier, in 1961, I had tried to get big businessmen to come in with me, but they told me frankly why they didn't like the proposition. They knew the Titans were losing about $100,000 a week, they did not like the Polo Grounds, and they had no assurance that the AFL would survive its fight with the NFL. I had to admit they had a case. We were not dealing in shoe factories, however, but in the risk business of sports. They had no foresight; I had too little cash.

Some few offers were insulting, such as the one made by M. Donald Grant, a one-time hotel clerk who is now a partner in Fahnestock & Co. and is Mrs. Charles S. Payson's man on the New York Mets. One night in the fall of 1962 Grant came over to the Park Lane Hotel to see me with George Weiss and Jim Thompson, both of the Mets. Grant had the audacity to offer me $250,000 for the Titans. I could not even begin to pay my bills at that price. I thanked Grant for his gesture, but told him I could do without him. It gave me pleasure to turn Grant down. He is an officious little man, strutting and pompous.

A business scare in the spring of '62 didn't help my case. President John F. Kennedy threatened to act against Big Steel in April if price increases were not rescinded. The former prices were restored, but the interplay left businessmen wary. Money went into hiding.

Then in late May the New York Stock Exchange had its worst one-day break in prices since 1929, with over $20 billion lost. There was a sharp recovery of about 65 percent the next day, but confidence had been hurt.

To pile it on, the Cuban affair exploded in the fall. It just wasn't a good year for risking money in sports. John Roosevelt, a Titan vice-president and a high executive in Bache & Co., made one last try to raise some money, but had to admit the task was hopeless. Roosevelt's verdict marked the beginning of the end because I did not have the money to go to camp in 1962 and I had no apparent means of raising additional funds. Then I had a bright idea. Why not consult Howard McCullough of Chicago? He was a generous man, well-known on the sports scene, who had set up many baseball and football players in the bowling business in his role as sales manager for the Brunswick Co. He also was a director of the Mercantile Bank in Chicago and might have some ideas about money sources.

I informed McCullough that I already had pledged all the collateral in my possession, but he pursued the subject. He inquired about future expectations, and I told him we were going to get up to $200,000 from the television contract. McCullough arranged to let me have $200,000 immediately in exchange for the rights to my television payments. These were delivered to the Mercantile Bank from October through January, in four installments, and totaled $190,000. I made up the remaining $10,000 and interest.

The money ran out on our opening trip to the Coast for an exhibition at San Diego and for two regular-season games at Oakland and San Diego.

Losses amounted to about $175,000. As we returned I was trying desperately to find money to pay the players and to raise the guarantees for incoming teams. But I was beaten. I called up Milt Woddard, the assistant commissioner, to tell him that unless I received substantial help, and quickly, I was finished. There was no help.

The AFL stepped in and operated the Titans from November 8 to the end of the season, but I, of course, still held the franchise, and sums paid out by the league were charged against me. As the 1962 season closed, I was disillusioned and bitter with my associates, and for good reasons. I had spent a considerable sum in behalf of the league without ever filing an expense account. I ran through more than $50,000 while setting up the television contract and selling sponsor space, and my bill for travel and entertainment on strictly league matters amounted to many additional thousands of dollars. There was no appreciation or consideration from my co-owners when I got in the jam; I was told only that Werblin would make a deal with me.

Adams, particularly, surprised me by his coldness; he had struck me otherwise as a genuine sportsman who would not let a partner sink without at least inquiring about his predicament, even if he could not assist him. Hunt, for all his wealth, never did impress me. Judge Thomsen had pointed out that Hunt, by his own admission, had been devious.

In January of 1963 I made a countryside tour visiting business men I had known for years, hoping to interest them in the Titans, but none cared to participate. When I had helped Bert Bell round up sponsors for NFL television, many of these same men turned me down then. Later, they begged to get on board at any price. Now they had turned me down again. I wonder whether they regret their decisions today. All they had to do was fight through 1963 and then the riches of Shea Stadium would have rewarded them.

On January 4, 1963, I entered into an agreement to sell my stock to the AFL for $1 million plus the sums advanced for operation since November 1, 1962, provided I did not find a purchaser of all or part of my holdings by the end of March.

At this time my losses amounted to $3.2 million, but I could cover only $2.1 million. In the second season of 1961 the loss amounted to $900,000, for a total of $2.1 million, which I paid out. Then, up to the time of my agreement, additional losses of $1.1 million pushed the grand total to $3,200,000.

In my agreement with the league, any purchaser that I might find would have to assume debts and produce working capital of $500,000. The total would run about $1.6 million. To protect my interests to the fullest and to give me freedom to operate legally in my own way, I filed a petition in Federal Court under Chapter XI of the Bankruptcy Act on February 6. This petition is far different from one filed under Chapter X. In that case a man simply throws in the towel and lets his creditors sweat. Chapter XI enables a man to claim time when in debt in order to seek means to refinance and reestablish his business if he can find the funds.

I also received permission of the court to remain "debtor in possession" and got a restraining order to keep the AFL from "disturbing" the status of the club while reorganizing. At this time, accountants delivered to the court a financial statement listing Titan assets at $271,999 and liabilities at $1,341,000, leaving a deficit of $1,069,001.

Without money, tactics were futile, and the end came in the law offices of Chadbourne, Park, Whiteside and Wolff, on March 28. I was beleaguered by lawyers. There were my lawyers, the AFL lawyers, the lawyers of the syndicate buying the Titans, the lawyers of creditors, the lawyers of the Irving Trust, which had held my stock in escrow pending the destination of the franchise. The scene is not one I care to recall. One lawyer handed me a check for $1 million to pay for my franchise, and I endorsed it and passed it along to the lawyer of the Irving Trust for apportionment among my creditors.

The Titans, born for excitement and glory on the field, finally died in the mustiness of a law office. I guess I was the only mourner.

I stumbled out of the office, into a bar. It was empty; the smell of the whisky gagged me. Was this all I had left? I had been wounded before, but the cut never had been so deep. Out on the street again, I walked. Toward home—empty—my wife in Europe where I had sent her to avoid the shame and humiliation of the bankruptcy proceedings. Everything I can recall now seemed touched with ugliness—women on the streets

with uncombed hair, dirty children, finally a battered cab, its
driver dropping me off at the apartment. I sat in the darkened
rooms, beset alternately by waves of indignation, humiliation,
self-pity, unable to think clearly, unable to gather my forces.
I felt that I had run a long distance and was tired and lonely.

PART V

AFTER THIRTY YEARS . . .

I made many headlines in New York and around the rest of the country when I first brought my Titans to the Polo Grounds. My first major headline coup was the signing of Sammy Baugh as Titan coach. One other sure-fire headline-getter was the periodic challenge I flung at the New York Giants of the NFL and the ways in which I couched these challenges. I would always drop a remark here, a retort there, that the Titans could beat the Giants easily, that Al Dorow was as good a quarterback as Y. A. Tittle, that we'd beat the Giants by 40 points, and that the Giants were afraid to play us. I would also remind one and all that the quality of football in the AFL was equal to play in the National Football League and that the Houston Oilers and the San Diego Chargers could beat any team in the NFL.

I knew that if the NFL had picked up these challenges, we probably would have been handed our heads. My Titans could not have beaten the Giants of 1960, '61, and '62, nor could the AFL All-Stars have beaten the NFL All-Stars, nor Houston or San Diego have beaten Green Bay or Chicago. It was all a publicity gimmick. I acted as I did to bring the Titans to the

attention of the fans of New York. I owned the most important
franchise in the AFL and I wanted to get space on the most
important sports pages in the country. I was laughed at in the
press, ridiculed, but I expected that. I didn't mind it at all as
long as the stories were printed and the AFL and the Titans
reaped the publicity reward. We weren't going to get any
publicity from our play on the field, so we had to get it some
other way. The only other way to get it was to challenge the
Establishment.

Now I am on the outside looking in at the two leagues and
I wonder if the two leagues will ever get together. I have been
reading and hearing a lot lately about the fact that the AFL
is here to stay; that the NFL had better recognize the AFL
soon and play the new league now when it can be fairly sure
of a victory because soon the AFL will achieve personnel parity
with the NFL. I don't think that's true. The NFL has nothing
to gain by playing the AFL and moreover, I am not sure that
the AFL is going to survive. Those who say that the AFL is
here to stay base their statement primarily on the lucrative
NBC television contract that the league was awarded last year.
The contract begins taking effect during the 1965 season and
it is supposed to run for five years, with a reputed $36 million
to be paid over that stretch of time only if NBC can sell enough
sponsors to carry AFL football and pick up the tab. But last
year the AFL's rating fell disastrously. Of course, 1964 was the
last year of the ABC contract, but in their championship game
in Buffalo, the winning Buffalo Bills only received $2,668 a man
and the losing San Diego Chargers, $1,738. The AFL will con-
tinue to ride along for a while on television revenue, but it
must build up greater national interest in its product or even
the television people will pull in their horns.

Television sponsors don't waste their money on shows that
don't draw, and although pro football is the product and it's

a proven commodity via the NFL, the decreasing interest in AFL football on television over the past four years indicates that the league had better do something to step up its TV image.

The AFL has one glaring weakness—only half of its franchises have any real fan support. In the NFL the Cardinals have not drawn too well in St. Louis, nor have the '49ers in San Francisco, but St. Louis will pick up when the new stadium is opened. All the '49ers need is a few more good football players.

The AFL has strong franchises from the standpoint of fan support in Buffalo, Boston, and New York, with Houston relatively strong. The Jets benefitted from the move to Shea Stadium to such an extent that their attendance in 1964 was the best in the AFL. The year before the Jets had played in the Polo Grounds and found attendance there no better than I had found it during my three years with the club in the same park. But the Western Division teams of the AFL have absolutely no fan appeal in the East, and they don't even draw particularly well in their own towns. San Diego is a fairly good draw on the road, but again only in the eastern cities.

In Minneapolis in 1959, George Halas almost put us out of business before we could begin. He took us out of the Midwest, which may be almost as bad. I tried to convince my former colleagues that football is played in other places besides Texas and California. I explained to them over and over that we needed two franchises in the Midwest—one in Chicago and the other in Detroit or Cleveland. Even if we didn't get one in Detroit or Cleveland we should at least have established one in Chicago. Midwesterners have been nurtured for decades on the great football rivalries between the Lions, Bears, Packers, Cardinals, and Browns. Now the young Minnesota Vikings have established a solid rapport with their fans and Metropolitan

Stadium features sellout crowds for every Viking home game. The Vikings are an exciting young team and one that will be heard from in the next few years.

But the AFL is sitting on both Coasts—with nothing in between. Millions of football fans in the Midwest—and all they can watch is NFL football. If Joe Foss wants to do something for the AFL, he should convince the owners to expand into that area. But expansion for the AFL means a serious cut in TV revenues. Instead of expanding they should move a franchise into Chicago. Lamar Hunt's Kansas City Chiefs, with some of the best personnel in the AFL, should be the ones to move. Hunt pulled out of Dallas, his home town, when he found out that Murchison's Dallas Cowboys were outdrawing him, and I know he has no sentimental attachment to Kansas City. The transplants would probably have to play in Soldier Field, but Soldier Field could be remodeled to hold 60,000 or 70,000 people, and the fans could be seated close to the field, not half a mile away as they used to be when the Rockets of the AAFC were playing there. If the AFL tries to move Oakland or Denver into the Chicago area, however, it will be a big mistake. The Chicago football fan is one of the most sophisticated, if not *the* most sophisticated, in the country, and he wouldn't support a second-rate team. If the AFL is to go into Chicago, it is going to have to go in with a very strong team, because it will have to compete with George Halas and the Chicago Bears. Nobody yet has beaten Halas and his Bears in Chicago, and only Charlie Bidwill's Cardinals of '47 and '48 ever made any serious inroads on Chicago's fandom.

The AFL has been talking about expansion, but I think they would be seriously mistaken if they were to move into other cities without having a more attractive product to sell from their original group. The NFL, however, can profitably expand into at least two more cities. They have strong franchises all around the country and going into areas like Atlanta or New

Orleans would certainly add strength to the string. If they did expand into two more areas, they would achieve the eight-club setup that Halas has hoped for. You couldn't imagine a more impressive league. The East would include New York, Cleveland, Pittsburgh, Philadelphia, Washington, Baltimore, and, say, Atlanta and New Orleans. The Western Division would include Green Bay, Chicago, Detroit, St. Louis, Minnesota, Los Angeles, San Francisco and Dallas. New Orleans, particularly, would make an atractive addition. For years I did the Sugar Bowl games in New Orleans and it is a great football town. The AFL was down there last January to play their All-Star game and the advance ticket sale for the game was tremendous. Because of the unfortunate situations that led some of the Negro players to feel they were being discriminated against, the players withdrew from the All-Star game and it was played in Houston. I feel that the Negro players had every right, if there were discriminatory practices, to pull out of the All-Star game. However, I think that commissioner Foss should have been on the scene and taken an active role in trying to resolve the problem to the satisfaction of all concerned. The responsible citizens of New Orleans apologized profusely to the AFL and to the players. If Foss had been there instead of on the road, fishing and hunting, or whatever he was doing, he might have saved the game for New Orleans. The AFL had made a commitment, the New Orleans people had delivered, almost everyone was trying to work out an amicable arrangement, and had it been played, the game would have introduced the AFL to the Southland and the vast market that is available down there. Now, after the pullout, New Orleans is ripe for the NFL and the older league should have no problem moving into the area if it wishes to do so. The promoters for the AFL All-Star game took a real beating but it wasn't their fault. An exhibition game in New Orleans last summer showed what kind of football support the NFL can expect when, for the third straight year, over 65,000 people came to the Sugar Bowl to see the game.

When I was still with the AFL, I made a suggestion to my colleagues which they turned down in their usual manner. I think the same suggestions made today would receive somewhat more attention. The AFL is a television league. Its support comes from television and not from the gate. It follows, then, that the AFL should do everything possible to maximize its television exposure and to increase the opportunities for sponsors to buy time during the games. They should change their scheduling of games from September to December to an October through January arrangement. If the AFL were to begin its regular season games after the World Series and carry the schedule through January, it would assure itself of two things: one, no conflict with the World Series; and two, a better opportunity for more sponsors to invest in the games. The question of weather would certainly enter into the picture, but the schedule could be arranged so that the last part of the season could be played in the West and Southwest and the early portion of the schedule could be played in the East. For instance, the Jets could be scheduled at Shea Stadium through October and November, and then travel during December and January. This arrangement would take advantage of the relatively decent weather in New York in the early fall and also offer more football to more sponsors and a large viewing public in December and January. The championship game could be played in a western park such as San Diego or the new stadium in Oakland. Moreover, with this type of schedule, the AFL could steal a march on the NFL, whose owners and leadership are eightly bound to the traditional September beginning. The AFL would start to pick up some NFL fans, since the NFL season would be over and the pro football fan, being the type of animal he is, would still rather watch football on Sunday afternoons than anything else. The AFL would be impinging on the basketball and hockey seasons, but after all, pro basketball and hockey begin in October, right in the middle of the football season, so why not extend the football season into the heart of the basketball and hockey seasons?

I doubt if there is much to be said for the possibilities of a merger between the AFL and the NFL. Though the AFL and NFL war hasn't been as bitter as the NFL-AAFC war was in the late Forties, there is really little reason for the NFL to merge since the AFL hasn't hurt them at the gate nor is it eating into the NFL's television revenues. The AFL maintains that the public demands a meeting between the champions of the respective leagues. The players are demanding a meeting between the two leagues for the benefit of their pension fund. But from what I know of the way football operates, neither the fans nor the players will have very much to say about it. This is strictly a business proposition. The NFL has nothing to gain by playing the AFL and I am sure the NFL owners will not agree to a meeting since it would mean recognizing the rival league.

Last January the National Collegiate Athletic Association came out and criticized professional football for signing players who still had eligibility remaining. Most of the players involved were bowl-bound seniors, but in some cases they were juniors with a season left to play, but eligible for the draft. Pete Rozelle, commissioner of the NFL, moved immediately to impose a stiff fine on any club found to have tampered with a college player's eligibility, but my old friend Joe Foss was still bumbling around a month later before he finally agreed to enforce the same rule in the AFL. The NCAA's request that the pros recognize the amateur status of their college players is certainly understandable, if somewhat hypocritical. The competition between the AFL and the NFL for players is mild

compared to the competition between colleges for star high
school performers. These players, when they reach college,
attract hundreds of thousands of fans who pay millions of dollars to see them play. When the chance comes for them to
dicker with the pros for their services, they should be permitted every opportunity to do so.

I don't think the pros should be permitted to negotiate for
them in the middle of the season, but a definite arrangement
should be established. It would seem to me that the NCAA
and the pros could work out a schedule for the second week
in December. In this way, boys whose teams have qualified for
a bowl game would not suffer financially by having to forsake
negotiating with the pros while fulfilling their obligations to
their schools. It is difficult to see how a bowl-bound team or
the school could suffer. These negotiations are conducted on
the campus and usually consume no more than a few days. The
publicity about a player's signing could have a very healthy
effect on the eventual gate for a post-season game.

If I had to point to the one area in which the NFL com-
pletely overshadows its younger rival today, that area would be
coaching. Twenty years ago a genius named Paul Brown entered professional football as coach of the Cleveland Browns.
Before his arrival, only one other man had ever devoted his
full efforts, twelve months of the year, to football, and that
man was George Halas. (One of the reasons Sammy Baugh
and I parted company was that Baugh was unable to perform
as a full-time coach for me.) Halas' and Brown's records speak
for themselves, and are reflected in the attitudes and proce-
dures of the NFL coaches today. There are many capable people in the AFL today but none who compare with their NFL
counterparts. The ranking genius of the NFL today is Vince
Lombardi of the Green Bay Packers. Lombardi's achievements
are well documented in the official record books of the NFL

and in the countless newspaper columns and magazine articles that have been written about him, but pro football has not seen, with the exception of Paul Brown, a man with the organizational genius that Lombardi possesses. If the reader wants to get the inside look at football from the players' and coaches' standpoint, he could do no better than to read Lombardi's classic book *Run to Daylight*, written with W. C. Heinz. There is no one in the AFL who can match Lombardi and none probably can match his colleagues either. If it survives, the AFL may some day achieve a parity with the NFL as far as playing personnel goes, but it will take a long time before it achieves equal status in the coaching ranks. Lombardi, intelligent, tough, and single-minded, reflects the entire NFL roster of coaches—Tom Landry in Dallas, Allie Sherman in New York, Don Shula in Baltimore, Norman Van Brocklin in Minnesota and, of course, George Halas and the others. Perhaps Sid Gillman of the San Diego Chargers and Weeb Ewbank of the Jets come closest to ranking on a par with the coaches in the NFL, but both are former NFL coaches and are schooled in NFL methods.

In the May 9, 1965, edition of the *New York Herald Tribune*, Harold Rosenthal carried the story about Sonny Werblin's refusal to let his two prize quarterback prospects, Joe Namath and John Huarte, participate in any pre-season All-Star games. Mr. Werblin seems to think that he is independent of AFL obligations. The AFL along with the NFL has a contract with the *Chicago Tribune*, which promotes the All-Star game, to permit players selected by the *Tribune* to participate in the All-Star extravaganza. Werblin said that he didn't want to run the risk of injury to his boys and that his decision would stand, regardless of what Joe Foss said. Whatever Foss said, however, was enough to make Werblin back down. Huarte will play with the All-Stars. Namath's playing was never an issue. I learned, from an unimpeachable source at the *Chicago*

Tribune, that the *Tribune* never wanted Namath on the All-Star squad. Indeed, they would have refused to accept him under any circumstances.

The AFL is nonexistent in the Midwest. If an owner of one of the clubs in the AFL had refused to permit his draft choices selected for the All-Star Classic to participate, he would simply have sunk the AFL a little lower in the opinion of midwestern fans. Werblin believes that the All-Star game is archaic. I beg to disagree with him. Many fine college football players who were not drafted by the pros have come up with great showings in All-Star games and were able to win good contracts and go on to become successes in professional football. I need only refer to Ron VanderKelen of Wisconsin, who led the 1963 All-Stars to a stunning win over the Green Bay Packers. VanderKelen had been drafted by me and not the NFL, but after his remarkable performance in the Rose Bowl game against USC and later in the All-Star game, he signed with the Vikings. But with or without VanderKelen's example, the College All-Star game has been a great curtain-raiser for the football season.

In the Thirties, the pros used it as a device to establish themselves nationally. Now, in the Sixties, when the pros have taken over and dominate the football news, it is their obligation to maintain the All-Star game in all its glory and spirit. Without exception, every boy who plays in the All-Star game, or in any football game, for that matter, runs the risk of injury. But they are also proud to be selected, and it means a lot to the local pro fans to catch a preview of some of the boys who may be starring on their team for years to come. The fact that Werblin thinks he is above the fans, who loyally support this game, and the players, both pro and collegiate, who are donating their services, is indicative of the type of thinking so prevalent in sports today by owners of major league franchises.

Three years ago, when Barron Hilton brought Werblin into the AFL to take over our television operations, his only knowledge of football was what he saw on television. Now, a few years later, he is an "expert" on every ramification of the game. Sonny seems to have forgotten two important things. First, in the end the fan is the one who counts. Second, the chances of Huarte being severely hurt in this game are minimal; the chances of his emerging a hero are considerably higher. If Huarte is the star, it will mean that much more in establishing the idea that the AFL is gaining stature. And think of the stories the next day about Sonny the Seer, who was clever enough to have signed not only Huarte but Namath as well, and of the wonder team he is building around them.

Werblin should stop thinking about himself and for once give something back to the league. After all, he got my franchise for a song and should at least recognize that he has more than just an obligation to the New York fans and himself; he has an obligation to his league and to all of football. I'd let Namath and Huarte and anybody else play if I still had the ballclub. Pro football owes much to the College All-Star game and should never forget it.

Owners today in pro football and baseball have begun to show a distressingly common lack of regard for the fans. The imminent movement of the Milwaukee Braves to Atlanta is probably the most flagrant exhibition of carpetbagging in the last five years, ranking second only to Walter O'Malley's move for the California gold back in 1958. In both cases, the fans had supported the teams involved loyally. But the riches of the Coast and of the South were too great for the owners to resist, and so they turned their backs on the fans who had supported them through good times and bad. For the last thirteen years, the Braves have had the highest average attendance per season in the National League. The year O'Malley pulled

the Dodgers out of Brooklyn, they drew over one million fans
to tiny Ebbets field.

O'Malley and his Dodgers and the syndicate that owns the
Braves can pack up and move to wherever they want because
nobody speaks for the fans. The commissioner, Ford Frick, has
been nothing but a rubber-stamp for the owners. It is true that
the commissioner draws his power only from the owners and
his job exists only as long as the owners vote him into office.
His contract with the league has to be renewed every seven
years. However, the commissioner has one great weapon on
his side, and that is the weapon of public opinion. Anyone with
common sense and empathy for the fans can see that the Milwaukee move is nothing but a grab by a group of cash-minded
businessmen for a financial killing at the expense of the people
of Milwaukee. Frick and the rest of the owners should have
stopped it. (The fact that they didn't is not so much a com-
mentary against the owners of the Milwaukee franchise as it is
against the rest of baseball.) These people who took over the
Milwaukee franchise are from Chicago. They have no ties with
Milwaukee and couldn't care less about the support it has given
the team in the past. They see in Atlanta a huge pile of television and commercial riches. Their television contract didn't
bring in enough revenue as far as they were concerned, but
down in Atlanta they will have the entire South to exploit. And
exploit they will. If the South dries up in four or five years as
a baseball El Dorado, these people will pack up and go to some
other place. In fact, we may see this same franchise move again
and again in the next twenty years. As long as there is television to pick up the tab, who cares about the fan!

And what can the fan do? He writes complaining letters to
the editor, he pickets the ball park, he refuses to attend the
ballgames, and he berates the ownership. But the fans don't
sell the radio and TV rights. The fan has nothing to say about
baseball these days and baseball is the weaker for it. If these

owners are permitted to pack up and move to another area as soon as attendance drops off a bit, baseball will soon degenerate into a traveling road show. There are still a few solid franchises in baseball, but when certain strong owners like Tom Yawkey of the Boston Red Sox, Phil Wrigley of the Chicago Cubs, and Bob Carpenter of the Phillies pass on or sell their franchises to syndicates, the game of baseball musical chairs probably will grow even wilder and more ludicrous than it is today.

There has been a great deal written about the movement of different baseball franchises and almost without exception the sports writers are against this kind of wandering. But putting this issue on a business basis, which is something that even the baseball people should understand. It becomes even more apparent that the movement of franchises becomes not only a disaster for the local area but weakens the entire financial structure of the league as well. A recent column by Red Smith puts it best:

Baseball people have never discovered that they are business partners. They see a lodge brother losing his shirt in a bush-league operation and don't realize that he is stripping them to the waist, too. The league president does not raise his voice to protest the despoliation of a city and a territory. The baseball commissioner does not lift a finger.

The other owners say, "It is his business." It is their business, too. The welfare of every club should be the president's direct concern, since what is bad for one is bad for all. "It is a league affair," the commissioner says, but when a fertile baseball territory is ravished, it should be baseball's affair.

What the carpetbaggers in baseball have done to Milwaukee is tragic, but the tragedy is magnified even further when you think of the reaction of the average fan to this move. Baseball needs the support of the fan. It has had his support for

years and has done nothing to insure its continuation. It has
frittered away the good will of the public through a series of
heavy-handed moves, and the Milwaukee transfer is just another page in the same long, dreary story. If the trend con-
tinues, baseball may find itself struggling with wrestling for
the low spot on the totem pole of sports—and I don't mean to
insult wrestling.

Baseball's handling of television is another monument to its
managerial stupidity. By permitting major league games to be
televised into minor league areas, baseball cut off its lifeline,
the flow of fresh young talent to the majors, and drove the
minor league fan away from the ballpark to his television set.
One of the best examples of baseball's amazing ability to alien-
ate itself from the public was the recent fiasco in New York.
The Jets of the American Football League were scheduled to
play an exhibition game with the Boston Patriots at Shea Stadium in late August of 1965. The proceeds from this game, an
estimated $100,000, would go to the Police Athletic League.
However, the baseball Mets, under the astute guidance of
Donald Grant, moved to have the Jets, their co-tenants, restrained from playing their exhibition game because "it would
ruin the field for baseball."

The Mets were to be out of town for a two-week period
during which the football game would be played, and the
groundskeepers and everyone concerned with the maintenance
of Shea Stadium insisted that the field would not be damaged
in the least by one football game. After all, in Cleveland the
Browns play an exhibition doubleheader in the middle of
August and the Indians are back playing baseball four days
later. In Milwaukee, the Packers play in Milwaukee County
Stadium on a Saturday and the Braves appear there the following Tuesday.

But the Mets refused the Jets the use of the field. The matter
came to a head, and the Mets and the Jets met with Ford Frick

to iron out the problem. The commissioner in this case was the final authority and he was to arbitrate all disputes between the tenants. Naturally enough, the commissioner found for the baseball Mets. The whole episode received scant coverage around the country, but it is an indication of the way things happen in baseball. The Police Athletic League, whose people work tirelessly for the betterment of the youth of New York, needed this $100,00. The Mets will try to soothe the PAL by selling $10,000 to $15,000 worth of tickets for PAL benefits, but that's a far cry from the $100,000 that would have been raised by the game. The baseball field would not have suffered, but the Mets' image has. If the Mets had any talented public-relations people working for them besides Casey Stengel, they would have seen the value of allowing the Jets to play their exhibition game, because the money that would have accrued to the PAL is far more important than the condition of a field. There certainly isn't going to be any World Series played in Shea Stadium for years to come, and the field could certainly have been restored to top condition for National League play in the time available. Besides, the Mets might have benefitted from a few divots here and there in the outfield and infield. They haven't done very well under ideal playing conditions.

Over the years I have had many good friends among the nation's sporting press. The vast majority of writers make every effort to be objective and truthful reporters. When I have been rapped, I undoubtedly deserved it. And when I was complimented, I was grateful. But when I became owner of the New York Titans and co-founder of the AFL, I became a victim of what I consider to be one of the foulest uses of the nation's sporting pages ever perpetrated. I was singled out by two writers in New York who for some reason had made up their minds to use me as a whipping boy for everything that was wrong with professional football, the AFL, and New York City.

Even today, two years later, I can read these columns and
bristle.

The men, Harold Weisman and Dan Parker, both of the now
defunct *New York Mirror* went out of their way to attack me.
I have never met Dan Parker and can recall meeting Weisman
only once—at a cocktail party I threw for the New York football
writers. Neither of these two writers ever interviewed me,
ever came to my home to talk with me, ever took the time to
get to know me, and yet they deliberately and maliciously used
their columns to attack and humiliate me.

I have shown these columns of Weisman and Parker to
friends of mine, including some lawyers, and the lawyers particularly have said that I probably would have had a pretty
good case in court. But I had other, far weightier things on my
mind in those days and always have been somewhat immune
to innuendo and insinuation anyway, so I did nothing.

I had heard from other newspaper friends of mine that Dan
Parker was considered by most of them to be a first-rate person.
I had read Parker for years and he had never rapped me nor
criticized me. It was not until my break with Marshall that
Parker and Weisman began to pour on the vitriol. I later found
out that Parker was a neighbor of Tom Gallery, and maybe
their relationship had something to do with it, for both Marshall
and Gallery had sworn to break me. I don't know, maybe my
own actions as owner of the Titans and founder of the American
Football League triggered Weisman's and Parker's attacks.
None of the other writers followed their line, however, although
many of them took shots at me, and used me to develop a lot
of good copy.

Well, I am out of football now and Weisman and Parker are
out of the newspaper game. After the *New York Mirror* folded
a few years ago, Parker caught on briefly with the *Journal-
American,* and then retired. Weisman is now with the New
York Mets in a public relations capacity. What I said about
Casey Stengel a few pages back still goes.

I have always been aware of the value of a good press, and during my whole career in broadcasting and in football I have always maintained a good relationship with sportswriters. I like them. There is probably no more interesting a group of people in any other journalistic field. They make good companions and fast friends and I am proud to number many of them among my closest associates.

"Well, Charlie, what really happened on that play was that the center released for a drive block on the middle Sam Wamba while the right cornerback free-saftied into the flat zone where they were running a ZXZ end pattern and the right tackle pulled on a Blue Red 39 to take the blitzing red dog."

To the uninitiated ear listening to a professional football broadcast these days, that message would sound like the launching of a moon rocket. What the color announcer is simply telling the play-by-play announcer is that the fullback gained two yards off right tackle. That may be an extreme example of today's play-by-play announcer reporting a football game, but it probably isn't too far off the mark. Today broadcasters work as a team—the play-by-play man and the expert color man who dissects the "inside" of each play for the listener or both listening and viewing audiences. Some of these color men have become so expert that they can anticipate the kind of play a quarterback will call and tell the fan what to watch for. Sometimes they are right.

Sports broadcasting has improved considerably since I first began at WJR in Detroit. The physical equipment itself makes for major advances, and the versatility and imagination that directors sometimes show in using this equipment often borders on the astonishing. The isolated-camera device is certainly one that has added a broad new dimension to sports, especially football. Instant slow-motion shots of everything from Jack Nicklaus' drives to Lou Groza's field goals is another.

But the key to interesting programming is still the announcer.

He makes the show, especially the broadcast. I would rank today's crop of announcers as equal to their predecessors in the Thirties and Forties. I don't think there are any today who have achieved the star status reached by such past greats as Ted Husing, Bill Stern, Graham McNamee or, to come closer to the present, Mel Allen and Red Barber. Today's trend toward regional broadcasting of all but the major sports events works against the top announcers who are known nationally. A few men, like Chris Schenkel and Lindsey Nelson, are known and heard across the country and have firmly established their reputations, but the list is not long.

But if regional broadcasting has eliminated the star system, it has also created many more job openings for sportscasters. Today, a major league baseball club is considered second-class if it doesn't have at least three or four men in the booth. Many of these men are former ballplayers themselves, and in addition to trying to keep the viewing audience informed, they must sell the sponsor's products, conduct interviews, appear at charity benefits, at commemorative functions, and in general spread themselves rather thin.

Quite a few former pro ballplayers have made the transition from player to broadcaster rather easily. But not many have achieved the same success and stature they enjoyed as athletes. Paul Christman, former Chicago Cardinal quarterback, has done an outstanding job working with a real pro, Curt Gowdy, on the AFL games. Christman knows his business thoroughly and never confuses his presentations with too much technical jargon. Phil Rizzuto is fast becoming a top play-by-play announcer in baseball, and if Phil can keep his objectivity about the players or managers, he'll soon rank with the best. Of course, he has the Yankee network and CBS and an almost automatic World Series spot, so he should continue to grow and develop. Tom Harmon also has made a great name for himself in broadcasting. I love the work Joe Garagiola does, and he has a fine inside knowledge of baseball. As Joe gets used to the

Yankee job, I'm sure he'll not be reaching for the quick jibe so often, although his wit has virtually become his trademark.

There are many other famous athletes who are now in the broadcasting business, and some will eventually make it as more than color men. Frank Gifford, the former Giant halfback, for example, is rapidly climbing the ladder with CBS and may soon be one of their top men.

The job of the play-by-play man differs considerably from that of the color man. The play-by-play man must make the game live, must impart a kind of drama to the contest, not dominate the scene nor distract his audience from what is taking place on the field. The color man, too, must inform, but in such a way that the technical information he is trying to impart will come across clearly and rapidly.

As I mentioned, I can think of no better "team" working today than Curt Gowdy and Paul Christman. Other top men in the business are Vin Scully, Russ Hodges, Van Patrick, Bob Elson, Jack Brickhouse. A new broadcasting team made its debut in 1965—Chris Schenkel and Bob Cousy working on the National Basketball Associations' "Game of the Week." Cousy is particularly refreshing as a color man because he utilizes his long background and familiarity with the game to analyze play and players and coaches objectively. Schenkel complements Cousy nicely. He never interrupts Cousy, even though play may be going on. He knows the viewer can see the action on the floor and realizes that Cousy's insights add a valuable new dimension to the fans viewing pleasure. I'm happy to see how effective Chris has become, because he is one of my friends, one I helped get started in the business.

But all sports broadcasters become captives of the club or league that pays them. This is the way the business operates. I know because I was one of the first of the broadcasting shils and one of the biggest. Objectivity is a luxury that few owners or leagues permit their broadcasters. The last possible hope for more objective sports reporting in radio and television was the networks themselves, but even they have capitulated. They regard sports as entertainment, not news, and have relinquished to the sports writers the burden of objective reporting. But sports *is* news. More newspaper space in this country is given over to sports than to any other single area of news. This may or may not be a laudable circumstance, but it is a fact. The public wants to read about sports and it trusts the reporters who provide the stories. If sports columnists were employed by club owners, honest, critical, objective reporting would vanish and a necessary watchful eye would be removed from the sports scene.

Would a network, say NBC, permit David Brinkley to become associated with, or otherwise commit himself to, a company that sponsored his program? Of course not. But the networks do permit club owners to dictate who will broadcast their games. And woe to the announcer who tries to keep up a semblance of objectivity under these circumstances. This spring, Pat Summerall, former place-kicking star of the New York Giants, was replaced as color man on the Giants broadcasts. He'll work for the Washington Redskins next year. The reason given for Summerall's dismissal was that he sometimes called plays before the Giants left the huddle! Since Summerall is a knowledgable football man, familiar with the Giant plays and patterns, his guesses were usually quite accurate. It was intimated that he was helping the opposition, no matter how inadvertently, and therefore had to go. Nonsense! Last year many people were critical of coach Allie Sherman and the Giants' front office for trading away Sam Huff and Dick Modzelewski; and the chorus of complaint swelled when the Giants went bad and the replacements for Huff and Modzelewski didn't develop as rapidly as Sherman had expected. This criticism probably unintentionally entered into some of Summerall's comments during the games and was resented by the Giant front office and the coach. So Summerall was banished.

I remember doing the Giants-Steelers game from Pittsburgh in 1952. The Giants took a fearful beating from the Steelers, 63-7. I've always had the habit as a broadcaster of giving the listener and the viewer the score about every minute or so. As the game progressed, I'd say, "And the score is now Pittsburgh 28, New York 0 or Pittsburgh 35, New York 0. Lynn Chadnois made a beautiful 28-yard run for the last touchdown." And so on, as the score mounted.

The following week the Giants played at home in the Polo Grounds and I arrived about three hours before the game to get ready. Tim Mara met me at the entrance to the booth and after exchanging greetings, he got to the point. "Harry, why did you keep repeating the score last Sunday? The game was bad enough without your reminding everyone how badly we were being beaten!"

"But, Tim," I said, "the public should be kept informed of the score. Many people tune in while a game is in progress and don't want to wait five or ten minutes to find out how the game is going."

"But did you have to keep telling everyone how bad it was?"

I didn't blame Tim for being upset; his club had been miserable. But the fact remains that the listeners had to be kept informed, and informed up to the minute.

The point to be made in any discussion about the responsibility of the broadcaster to the listener and to his employer is that his first loyalty goes to his employer. This is natural. But how much better, for sports and fans alike, if the networks would inform the leagues and the owners that they wanted broadcasters who would give straight, factual, unbiased accounts of games, broadcasters who would not be wide open to employer reprisal if they called things as they saw them. But the system, the same system under which I operated and from which I benefitted, would appear to be too strong.

There probably has never been a sport and a broadcasting

medium so perfectly matched as television and football, especially pro football. When the NFL came out of the bloody war with the AAFC, television was beginning to establish itself across the country, and boxing and baseball people were lining up to drink the gold that came from this new, seemingly miraculous, electronic fountain. The pro football magnates, guided by the astute Bert Bell, refused to succumb to the financial temptation and, as we have seen, turned the new medium to their own ends.

The path they chose was the correct one. Television's uncontrollable appetite has already seriously crippled boxing and baseball, and if not checked, could also critically injure pro football.

The public would like to see more football on television and the networks would be only too happy to oblige. Last year the NFL began to run the risk of over-exposure under the weight of its $28 million deal with CBS. There was an hour Saturday afternoon show hosted by Tom Harmon. Then on Sunday there was a fifteen-minute pre-game show, then the game, followed by a fifteen-minute scoreboard show, not to mention late evening and afternoon highlights of some of the games. All these features are interestingly done, but as the season wore on the NFL began introducing its "doubleheaders," the AFL was televising, even the Atlantic Coast League was televising.

The television season began with the college All-Star game during the first week in August and ended on January 17 in Houston. To many otherwise avid viewers, the championship game, the pro-bowl games, the playoff-bowl game, had become anticlimatic. How much exposure can pro football stand? Will the newly formed Continental League land a contract and join the bandwagon?

The asking price for the television rights to NFL football games will go even higher after the present contract runs out. The pact with CBS ends after the 1965 season, and the bidding will then be between CBS and ABC. ABC will certainly offer considerably more than the $28.2 million CBS paid in 1964. But CBS will not stand idly by and let the package slip through its fingers, so the bidding will be lively. I would estimate that the final price for the 1966–67 rights to the NFL games will range between $32-$35 million! Fifteen years ago, the networks could have had these rights for $100,000.

If the networks are going to pay these prices, then they will insist on even greater control of the product. They will demand more exposure in order to entice more sponsors to pick up the tab. But there are only so many games that can be played on Sunday. Perhaps a pro game or two on Friday evenings would be the answer. The NCAA would object and high school authorities would complain again, but this time perhaps the league would not back down.

Another device the network might use would be to increase the number of "official" time-outs, so that they can allot more air time to one-shot sponsors. Everything adds up to just one thing—overexposure. What is the answer? It lies with the owners and commissioners. Better to guarantee the long-time appeal of the sport than to settle for a quick buck and kill it off.

Much of the responsibility must settle with the commissioners. Their perspectives are league-wide; they are, or should be, the ones most intimate with the broadcasting and advertising ramifications of the problem. The NFL is headed by Pete Rozelle, a quite efficient and effective man. Though not in the mold of Bert Bell, Rozelle has a good grasp of many of the problems the league has faced and will be facing during the Sixties, and chances are that he—and George Halas— will handle the situation to the best interests of all concerned in the NFL.

The AFL has Joe Foss. I wish it had Milt Woddard. There isn't anyone in the league besides Woddard who has the experience and know-how to chart the correct course. Few of the owners, even after five years, have exhibited much grasp of their mutual problem. Football isn't their main source of income; their interests are wide-ranging and mainly personal, not common. The league has never spoken with a united voice. Of all the AFL figures currently on the scene, Milt Woodard would seem to be the best man to be in control at this critical time. The AFL "fact book" carries this tribute to Woodard: "Commissioner Foss, himself, paid Woodard the finest compliment at a time when the commissioner contemplated returning to an active life in politics. 'I would never leave the American League unless I knew it was in excellent shape,' Foss stated. 'With Milt Woodard as commissioner, I'd have no fears for its future.'"

I irritated Foss by constantly insisting on moving the AFL offices from Dallas to New York. The AP quotes Foss out of our San Diego meeting in January of 1962: "I'd quit if we moved to New York. I'd play out my option." There was always a good chance of our moving to New York. Bud Adams in 1961 walked out of a meeting, saying: "If we don't move to New York I shall resign." Billy Sullivan of Boston was for New York from the start.

In fact, no one wanted Dallas except Lamar Hunt, and when he surrendered Dallas to the NFL and moved to Kansas City, the AFL headqaurters were moved to New York for 1963. It's futile to argue against New York. There is in that city more chance for more exposure to more media for the dissemination of news and features than any place in the world.

At the San Diego meeting in '62, Sid Gillman was at sharp odds with Foss over league matters. At one time the commissioner was requested to leave the room, and Wayne Valley took the chair. Foss was recalled only at four or five in the morning, and I felt that his tenure was at stake. He stated that Rozelle was getting a new contract and that we had to make it look good for him, too. There was something in what he said; it would be poor publicity for us to fire our commissioner the day after the other league rehired its executive officer. So we rehired Joe.

There was one other situation involving Foss and myself that received a great deal of one-sided publicity—in his favor. That was his statement that he ought to strip me of my franchise for "conduct detrimental to the league," conduct involving our secret draft in November of 1961.

This statement was so absurd that Lamar Hunt felt impelled to reply: "That's such a broad thing. The commissioner is a hired official and can be fired. I don't know if an owner could be fired. It's a pretty radical thing. It would be like the owners telling me I had to move out of Dallas. There probably would be seven votes out of seven in favor, but I don't know that I'd have to move."

Let me explain the secret draft. Adams and Hunt rigged this draft, with the clubs working on the phone for days.

We had drawn Ernie Davis, the great Syracuse back who died of leukemia while under contract to the Cleveland Browns. About 4 A.M. I was roused out of bed by a writer who wanted to know whether I had signed Davis. Thinking the news had leaked from someone in Syracuse, I admitted that we talked to Davis but had not signed him. Then my caller stated that Foss had called off the draft. I explained that Hunt and Adams had organized the draft, and I felt that they should let me know in the event that it had been cancelled.

The writer pressed me to say whether I would desist in efforts to sign Davis. I explained again that I had selected Davis in a draft with fellow owners and that it stood as far as I knew. I was staying with Davis.

The story came out that I defied Foss, which was not true, in light of my knowledge. I certainly was not going to give up a tremendous prospect because of a report a writer had heard.

Well, Joe is still the commisisoner and I'm out of the league. Joe's a nice guy and a great war hero. We and our children owe

Foss and the rest of our soldiers a great debt. But as a football
commissioner, Joe doesn't show me very much.

My all-time football greats? I have a list of those I've seen
but such compilations strike me as rather meaningless, reflect-
ing, as they do, sentiment, regionalism, and the like. But let's
see what we can come up with.

The most talented single performer I have ever watched was
Sammy Baugh. The greatest passer the game has ever seen,
Sam was also a fine runner, an extraordinary punter (as George
Halas will attest), and one of the game's all-time best defensive
backs. Next to Baugh as a passer I would rank Sid Luckman.
Sid was a master of the long pass, a top strategist, and a re-
spected field general. Of the present-day crop of passers, my
nod goes to Johnny Unitas and Bart Starr. Y.A. Tittle, Otto
Graham and Bobby Layne were tops during the Fifties and
early Sixties.

I would rank Dutch Clark close to Baugh in all-around
ability. Clark combined intellect, passing skill, and superb running ability into an irresistible offensive package. Bill Dudley
was cast along the same lines.

Running backs? I never saw Jim Thorpe, but I often watched
Bronko Nagurski in action and I have never seen his equal for
straight-ahead power and drive. Bronko also was a great defensive tackle. In an open field, I don't think anyone will ever
equal George McAfee, although Cliff Battles comes close. I
haven't forgotten Jim Brown; Jim is in a class by himself.

I have seen many great linemen, but those that stand out
most vividly in my mind are Bulldog Turner and Joe Stydahar
of the Bears, Mel Hein of the Giants, Don Hutson of the
Packers, and, more recently, Gino Marchetti of the Colts, Joe
Schmidt of the Lions, and Bill Willis of the Browns. But how
could you fail to include the great Packer offensive and de-

fensive linemen of the early Sixties. You see the problem—the list is virtually endless.

People have often asked me, since I broadcast so many of their games, who some of my all-time Notre Dame stars would be. Again, the roll goes on and on—Carideo, Brill, Schwartz, Connor, Martin, Hart, Lujack, Bertelli, Miller, Brennan, Sitko, and Hornung.

And of all the thrills, all of the great performances, I have seen during my career, which stands out most sharply? Once again, an impossible question. Luckman and the Bears grinding the Redskins to powder in the 73-0 NFL championship game in 1940; Kyle Rote leading an underdog Southern Methodist University club to within a whisker of victory over mighty Notre Dame in 1949; Notre Dame ending Oklahoma's great winning streak, 7-0, at Norman, Oklahoma in 1957; and the classic Colts-Giants championship game of 1958. I could go on and on about the players and the games but they are all too familiar to football buffs.

Early in June 1965, the National Football League announced its intention to expand in 1966 to sixteen teams. High on their list of cities for expansion were Atlanta, New Orleans, Houston, Boston, and Miami. I discount the last two because Boston doesn't have the facilities for a NFL club and Miami has never proved itself a pro town. It's had two chances and failed. But Atlanta has an $18 million stadium ready for the Milwaukee Braves and they are primed for pro football. New Orleans has the Sugar Bowl and Houston, the Astrodome.

After the NFL announcement, the American Football League, led by Sonny Werblin and Joe Foss, also decided to expand and named Atlanta, New Orleans, Philadelphia, Chicago, and Milwaukee as prime areas. On June 8, the American Football League awarded an Atlanta franchise to the Cox

Broadcasting Corporation for a record $7.5 million. Joe Foss immediately announced that the AFL had beaten the NFL to Atlanta! Congratulations, Joe and Sonny!

But on June 9, a small problem developed. There seemed to be some question whether the Cox group would have the use of the new stadium! The Cox people had assured Foss and the AFL all was rosy and so Foss and Werblin and the rest approved the Atlanta franchise. However, one Pete Rozelle, commissioner of the NFL, was in Atlanta on June 8, talking to Arthur Montgomery, Jr. Mr. Montgomery is chairman of the Atlanta-Fulton County Recreation Authority which controls the civic stadium. It seems that he and Pete had a fine meeting that day and Pete told Art that the NFL would easily be able to expand into Atlanta by 1966. Mr. Montgomery's comments are not available but I imagine he allowed himself a brief grin.

One group that bid for an NFL franchise is headed by Lindsey Hopkins, the Coca-Cola heir, and a close friend of mine for twenty years. Others who are associated with Hopkins are John Macom, Jr., of Houston, one of the wealthiest of Texas oilmen; Tony Hulman, operator of the Indianapolis Speedway; Ogden Phipps of New York and Charles Bradshaw of Orlando, Florida. Interestingly enough, Mr. Montgomery is also President of the Atlanta Coca-Cola Bottling Company.

Shades of Minneapolis! The AFL may be taken again. Didn't Hunt and Foss and Hilton and Adams learn anything from Minneapolis? If the NFL comes into Atlanta and knocks the AFL off again, someone somewhere must wonder who in the AFL knows how to run a league! This book will be on press before the final decision is made so I can only speculate, but I'll make my bet now—it's the NFL in Atlanta. I have two reasons for this prognostication; one, the fans of Atlanta would prefer the NFL; and two, the NFL would give the new franchise the right to share immediately in television revenues and thus put it on a sound operating basis immediately.

The AFL will not permit new franchises to share equally in television revenues during their first two years in the league. During their third year, new franchises would receive approximately one-third to one-half the amount that the other clubs in the league are getting; not until they had been in the league for four years could new clubs expect to share equally in the television pie. This means that during its first two years of operation, a new franchise would have to struggle along on the basis of league gate receipts, and the league as a whole hasn't been drawing well enough for any new teams to survive on that basis. In addition, new franchises would have to put up $7.5 million merely to join the AFL. With this two-year restriction, the present owners amass all the TV money, require new owners to pay through the nose to join them, and still maintain the fiction of expansion. Talk about having your cake and eating it too!

Why should the AFL deliberately handicap new franchises? Why, with the experience of the NFL to profit from, have the current AFL owners imposed such drastic conditions on the admission of new franchises? The AFL is a television league and has survived solely on the basis of its TV receipts. Yet the league expects to admit new members and at the same time to deny them the one ingredient they need in order to survive. This is hardly a situation to breed mutual trust and respect.

What could the new AFL owners expect in terms of talent from the other clubs in the league? Forced to accept humiliating financial terms as a condition of entry, they could scarcely expect their cohorts to subsidize them with respectable players. Not that the NFL would stock their new franchises with super stars, but at least they would be operating from the beginning as equals, and the NFL owners and commissioner have learned their lesson well—the league operates for the benefit of all its member clubs.

The NFL's approach to expansion is big league in every way.

The AFL restriction on TV revenues to a new franchise is a good gimmick and was probably, I would guess, put forward by Sony Werblin as leader of the expansion movement because the AFL owners were afraid of the dilution of TV money. I think the plan will backfire and create more problems for themselves and the new teams.

The future owners of new franchises in the AFL have my best wishes, but if they will take a word from a person who has been up the creek before, they will insist on a fair shake of TV monies before agreeing to the present expansion terms.

Since I am betting Atlanta will fall to the NFL, I'll go all the way and say I think Houston will be in the older league by 1967. I'm forecasting Houston because of the Astrodome and the fact that Bud Adams, owner of the AFL's Houston Oilers, said his team will play at Rice University Stadium. That leaves the Astrodome without a major tenant after baseball season and I'm sure the NFL will be only too happy to correct that situation. When I was in the AFL, we all kept hearing Adams say to wait until the Astrodome was built and then the AFL would show the NFL something about drawing fans. Well, all I have heard and read recently makes it obvious that Adams won't be in the Astrodome. The NFL could be in there in 1967 with no trouble. With a NFL franchise in Houston and the Dallas Cowboys only a hundred or so miles away, the NFL may have the makings of a southwest Packer-Bear feud.

If I had the opportunity, would I buy into another club? The answer is yes; the excitement, the glamor, the money—everything that originally attracted me, is still there, even more so. And I still believe that the way I operated was essentially sound. I still believe that the Richards touch, the touch of the showman, is essential in an operation of any kind; but far more important is the idea that originally you must be willing to put into a team or franchise much more than you might eventually expect to take out. God knows I contributed more to my club, my franchise, than I ever received from it. As Sammy Baugh put it, I simply ran out of money. I could have used more time, and more support, too. Time would have given me the new stadium. Support, financial support, would have tided me over until the stadium had been completed. And let us not kid ourselves—it is the stadium that has been responsible for whatever success the Jets have enjoyed at the gate. The team cavorts in green and white uniforms now and some of the faces are different; but the performance is the same, the record not even as good as the one the Titans compiled in the Polo Grounds. With the exception of Larry Grantham and Matt Snell, the team boasts no standouts, especially when you strip the mystique of the middle linebacker from Wahoo McDaniel.

There is one thing I would do differently were I back in the game. I would be more discriminating in choosing associates— no more amateurs, no more fair-weather friends. The game is tough and is played by professionals on the field according to professional rules. It should be run by tough, dedicated professionals in the front offices, who also play by professional rules, but who, in addition, prescribe to the basic law of professional sports survival—all for one and one for all.

It's been good for me to be able to look back and see the panorama of this great sport as I lived it. I've had both the good and the bad and the former far outweighs the latter. Pro football and broadcasting have been my life and the friendships and accomplishments and frustrations and disappointments have all made it a wonderful experience. I'm going to be back in the business someday, this golden business the public calls sport.